Silent Night

Silent Night

A Memoir

Ann Darby Reynolds

CAPTAIN NURSE CORPS USN RETIRED

ISBN 9798582021551

Cover and book design by Claire MacMaster
    barefoot art graphic design
Editorial services by Renee Nicholls
    www.mywritingcoach.net

Printed in United States of America

Dedicated to the US Navy Nurse Corps
For 26½ years

Contents

Acknowledgments

It all started one Spring afternoon when Pat Thomas, a resident at RiverWoods Exeter, asked if I had written my story down yet. As usual, I said no. She had offered to help several times. However, this time I surprised myself and agreed to accept her help. She interviewed me for several hours, and my book began.

After the first draft, I decided not to continue. Later on, however, several friends encouraged me to continue working on my memoir. Specifically, I'd like to thank the following helpers.

My good friends Brenda and Jay Meehan from college, for their continued support on this memoir.

Rita Betournay and Kathy Shea Ouellette, who kept after me and were an immense help with editing and formatting.

Mal Argondizza, Sue Marcella, and Gary Ouellette, who were frequently on call and helped with the computer. Without them, I would still be at ground zero.

Renee Nicholls, my book editor, and Claire MacMaster, my designer, who each gave me valuable support throughout the publication process.

I would also like to thank Debbie Kane: Kane Communications; Jan Herman, retired Historian Navy Medicine; Thom Hindle, retired Curator of Woodman Museum; and Jennifer Croot.

Finally, I am grateful for my many friends—military and civilian—who were also a part of my life. You are not forgotten. All of you have my eternal thanks, because this book would never have made it to the final stage without you.

Prologue: Christmas Eve, 1963

My first Christmas back home in New Hampshire after starting active duty was in 1963. It was wonderful to see my family. I had ten days for leave, but it was really eight because two days were travel days. It was a very cold night, but inside all was warm and cheerful. The Christmas tree twinkled as my family and friends mingled. Around 8:00 P.M., I looked out the window and noticed the mail truck pulling up in front of our house.

"Could it be a late present?" I thought. But my roommates and I had agreed not to exchange presents.

The mailman walked up the drive, carrying an envelope. I went to the door and signed for it. It was a special delivery—for me. The envelope's return address was Naval Hospital Pensacola, Florida.

I carried the envelope into the living room and opened it. It was from my chief nurse. The letter inside read:

> *Dear LTJG Reynolds:*
>
> *Congratulations, you have orders to Saigon, Vietnam. Your official orders await your return. Enjoy the rest of the holiday with your family.*
>
> *Captain Veronica Bulshefski*

I stared at the letter. I had never heard of Vietnam. What happened to being sent to Spain, Italy, or Japan?

"What's so important that you're receiving a letter on Christmas Eve?" Mom asked.

"It's my new orders," I said.

"Where?"

I read the letter out loud.

"Where is Vietnam?" she asked.

"I have no idea."

"They're sending you someplace and you don't know where it is?" she asked, skeptically.

"Yes."

No one else in the room knew where Vietnam was either. My cousin Tom had heard of Vietnam but didn't know where it was.

"Get the encyclopedia," someone suggested. We found Saigon on a map of Vietnam.

"It's across the Pacific Ocean," I said, thinking, *"That's a long way from New Hampshire."*

My mother glanced at the map and burst into tears, rushing out of the room. And that's how it went for the next two days; just looking at me caused tears and she had to leave the room.

"Why am I being sent to Vietnam, a place I've never heard of that has no hospital?" I wondered.

I couldn't wait to get back to Pensacola to learn more.

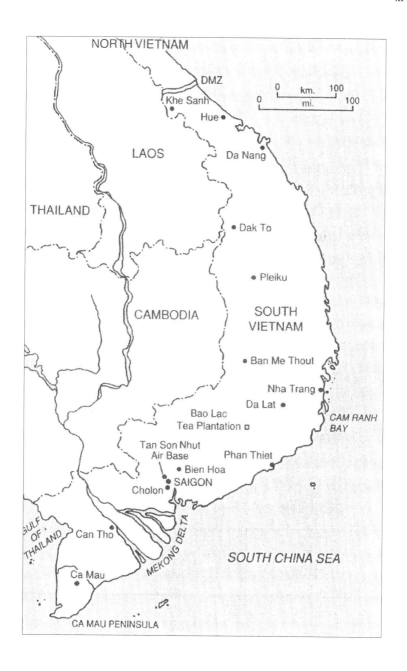

Chapter 1

Growing Up

I was born in Dover, New Hampshire, on September 12, 1939. My mother, Ann Reynolds, was of Irish and Scottish descent. She had liked the name Darby ever since meeting someone with the same name in Ireland, where she had visited family.

Darby and her mother, Ann Reynolds

My father, Francis (Frank) Reynolds, was raised in Dover by my grandfather, after my father's sister died very young of what was thought to be diabetes. After this tragedy, my grandmother went back to her family in Massachusetts and never returned. I never met her.

When I was born, we lived in my grandfather's big house on Maple Street in Dover—at the time a small city of 16,000 people. My sister, Ellen Frances, was born in 1941.

My father was in the U.S. Navy (Seabees) toward the end of World War II. He then went on and worked at the Portsmouth Navy Shipyard in Portsmouth, New Hampshire.

Since my mother was Ann and my grandmother (her mother) was also Ann, at home I was called Ann Darby. At school I was called Ann in kindergarten and throughout first and second grades, but at home I was still called Ann Darby. When Ellen was five, she asked, "Why do you have two names?" Soon after, someone in the neighborhood assumed Darby was my last name and asked if I was adopted. After that, both at school and at home I started to use my middle name, Darby.

* * *

When I was six or seven, I saw a ballet and decided to be a ballerina. I liked the dancer's beautiful white costume and her dancing, so my parents signed me up for a dance class. Not too long after I started practicing how to walk on my toes, I decided against being a ballet dancer.

There was, however, another class: tap dancing. I asked my parents to enroll me and I practiced all the time—tap, tap, tap, all through the house. My mother and father soon had enough, and they usually said, "Go practice on the porch." I often continued down the sidewalk to visit my neighbors; they called my mother and sent me home.

* * *

When I was about seven, I became fascinated with the majorette who was marching and twirling her baton during the Dover Christmas parade. I was in luck: my dance studio had a class for majorettes. I eagerly enrolled, got my baton, and was soon practicing my eights and circles, throwing my baton in the air and trying to catch it. One day I missed and broke my mother's favorite lamp; she then banished me to practice in the backyard. Nobody could see me, and the only damage I could do was to the trees.

One year, I was going to be in a parade on the Fourth of July. The American Legion sponsored our class of junior majorettes. Our outfits were sky blue and satin, and my mother made mine. My father, a member of the American Legion, was also in the parade. My mother and Ellen stayed home, as it would be too long a day for my sister. I was so excited I woke up very early.

The parade was in a city a few hours away. There were twenty majorettes in my group. Over and over we marched for a while and then paused in the street to do our program, throwing our batons in the air. Not everyone caught them, so we scrambled to find them on the road. Then everyone watching clapped, and we marched on to the next stop, paused, and performed again. I was soon tired and it was very hot—over ninety degrees. While I was waiting for the parade to move forward, I noticed a small group of kids around my age sitting on the curb, with their parents sitting behind them in chairs.

They were in the shade and it looked cool, so I left my twirling group to sit in the shade with them. The other kids liked my outfit and wanted to try my baton, so I let them. The parents even gave me some water. Then the parade started again. I was comfortable, so I decided to stay with my new friends and watch the parade. Near the end, I stood up and followed one of the marching groups.

They kept turning around to look at me. Two of the women from the women's auxiliary had noticed I was missing and were frantically searching for me. They found me and turned me over to my father. Once we got home and my mother found out, well, that's another story.

* * *

I think I originally learned how to ice skate because I roller-skated and liked it. My mother often took Ellen and me into Boston to see the Ice Capades and Ice Follies. I loved seeing the skaters. I had seen Olympic skater Sonja Henie on television and wanted to be like her. But since I was determined to be a great skater, I needed a place to practice.

There was no ice-skating rink in Dover, so my father and grandfather built a circular frame in our large backyard, packing down the grass and dirt. I didn't know what they were doing.

"Why don't you fill it with water?" I suggested.

Later the ground froze, and they put water in the frame. I had my ice rink! It wasn't long before the neighborhood kids discovered the rink, and I had plenty of company.

As the years passed, I got better at skating and outgrew my ice rink. By that time Dover had built an ice-skating rink, supposedly for "big kids." I skated up until high school. Once, in the ninth grade, I caught my skate in a crack in the ice at a local pond and fell, breaking my arm. Remember "the whip"—the person at the end of a string of skaters who got pulled around and went really fast? I liked being that person.

* * *

When I was in the first grade, I received a nursing kit with a stethoscope. I wanted to be a nurse like my Aunt Rose, who was a public health nurse for the state of New Hampshire. I often took day trips with my aunt in the summer, which gave my mother more time to spend with Ellen, who was often sick.

My aunt held clinics for new mothers and newborns. I helped her set up tables to get ready for the doctor. When the clinic was open, I usually went outside to play, although if it rained, I sat indoors with a book.

One day, the doctor asked me, "What do we have here—a young nurse in training?"

"Yes," I said. "I'm going to be like my aunt." I've always remembered that day.

After each clinic was over, I helped Aunt Rose put things away. Often she stopped to make a couple of house calls to see patients while I waited in the car and read a book.

In fifth grade I discovered the public library, and in the winter I often stopped there on my way home from school to get warm. Sometimes the librarian would help me find books about nurses. *Cherry Ames* was my favorite, and I read every book in the series. Every time a new *Cherry Ames* book came out, I decided I'd be a school nurse, a camp nurse, or whatever type of nurse she was in that volume (she even went overseas).

* * *

When I was in elementary school, I had two close friends: Carol, who lived one street over from me, and Elaine, who lived around the corner. We had activities to keep us busy after school and on weekends.

During school, I went home for lunch, and sometimes my mother and Ellen would meet me halfway. Most of the time I walked home alone. I liked most of my classes, and my grades were okay.

In fifth grade, my parents enrolled me at St. Mary's School, a Catholic school for boys and girls grades one through eight. Carol and Elaine didn't join me, but I met them again in high school. I walked a little over a mile to reach St. Mary's.

Sometimes after school, I walked up Central Avenue, stopping at Woolworths and the jewelry store. I loved looking at all the jewelry. I must have admired sapphires, because on my next birthday, my grandfather gave me a sapphire ring. I was spoiled.

I also loved Wonder Woman. She carried a bow and arrow, and I received one for another birthday. I was pretty good with it, and I practiced on the big target on our barn door.

We celebrated birthdays during the summer. My father's birthday and Ellen's birthday were in August; mine was in September. My mother's birthday was in November. We had cookouts with lots of people. My father would buy lobsters and clams, and we cooked them in the backyard. We used old sawhorses, topped by old doors, for tables and benches. My mother baked a chocolate cake.

Christmas was always special. We had a big, real tree and decorated it, and friends and family came over for Christmas Eve. I always helped make the turkey stuffing. We went to Christmas midnight Mass. There were lots of presents for everyone.

My aunts and uncle were often at the house, especially at the holidays. My other aunt, uncle, and two cousins lived in New

Jersey, and I went down to visit them for a few weeks each summer. I would return to New Hampshire with them when they came North for a month.

* * *

When I was in the eighth grade, my mother went to work as secretary for the mayor of Dover. One afternoon when she returned home from work, she held her hand up in the air and said, "You cannot touch my hand. No one can touch my hand. I have just shaken hands with the President of the United States, President Harry S. Truman."

President Truman came to New Hampshire to speak and stopped at the Dover mayor's office. He shook my mother's hand and asked her name—it was a big thrill for her. She loved her job and met many interesting people.

While I was in the eighth grade, we also moved from my grandfather's home to a house on Abbott Street. I did not want to move. We could not persuade my grandfather to move with us. Ellen and I had our own bedrooms, which were a lot larger than before. The new house was nice, but I missed my grandfather.

I had to give up my dog, too, since my mother was working and no one was at home to take care of him. He was a collie named Sir Shepherd of Nottingham (we called him Shep). We found a good home for him, but life wasn't the same.

Then I had to decide where to go to high school: continue on at St Mary's High School for Catholic girls, which was small, or move to Dover High, which was larger and had more college prep classes. Aunt Rose favored Dover High since I wanted to study nursing in the future, so that's where I went. I ran into my old elementary school friends and made many new ones. My friends Carol, Elaine,

Joe, and Annette were a large part of my life. Even today, we continue to remain in contact from our various coasts and meet up again at reunions.

* * *

By the time we moved to Abbott Street, we owned a summer cottage in York Beach, Maine, on Long Sands Beach. Long Sands is a family beach, and we could see the famous Nubble Lighthouse from the beach. Short Sands, the smaller beach about a half mile away, featured restaurants, a movie theater, and an amusement park. Our family had often rented places at the beach during previous years, and it was only about forty minutes from Dover. We also made many day trips from our home to this area.

I had many friends my age in Maine, and everyone was looking for adventure. One time, we walked over to the Nubble Lighthouse, which is on a small island off York Beach. There was a very low tide that day and a small area where there was hardly any water, so we decided to walk over on the narrow strip of sand to look around. From the mainland there were large rocks we had to climb down to get to the sand, and then once we were across, there were larger rocks to scramble over to get up to the grass on the island.

It was a great view, but then the tide changed and we had to hurry back. All but one of us managed to make it back across. Our other friend had to wait for the tide to change again, and then he was brought back to land in a boat by the lighthouse keeper. That tide was not low enough to walk.

During the summer of 1954, my father found a job for me. At the time, I thought it was the best job I had ever had. I was the "float girl." I rented beach chairs, umbrellas, and a rubber raft called the "float" to beachgoers. My job started when school ended in

June and we moved to the beach for the summer, and it continued through Labor Day. It was seven days a week, 8:30 A.M. to 5:00 P.M. The man who owned the concession brought all the chairs, umbrellas, and rafts down to the beach around 8:30 A.M. I set them up and he put up a few umbrellas, then left. He had three other stands on Long Sands and more on Short Sands. My spot was open until 5:00 P.M. when he collected everything, including money.

The job varied depending on the weather. If there was a shower, I waited until it was over to rent chairs and rafts. The only time I had off was if it rained all day. When Annette and other friends came to visit, we had to wait until I was free before going to Short Sands; they stayed on the beach all day. My mother and Ellen often relieved me for a short time if I wanted to go to the cottage.

When I rented a raft, I kept an eye on the people as they went out to ride the waves. There were several lifeguards along the beach, and they blew their whistles when people went too far. Sometimes they went out to bring someone back to shallow water. The waves weren't that high, but there was frequently an undertow. A neighbor who lived across the street from us in Dover drowned in the undertow one year. His two children were around my age. It was hard for our family as well.

The family of one of my high school friends, Jack, had a cottage next to ours. Jack and other friends often came to my stand to hang around, using my chairs and rafts to sit on. Frequently the owner drove by, checking his stands, and asked me to tell them to move.

"People won't rent with that crowd," he said. I always told the group to move, but a few hours later they came back. At least they helped me pass the time since we were all the same age.

On rainy days when I didn't have to work, I often sat on the steps to the beach, where I watched the waves break against the shore and listened to the foghorn. I liked looking at the lighthouse, the big ships, Boone Island, and the Isles of Shoals. Sometimes I wondered what was on the other side of the ocean, and what it was like to be on a big ship. I loved it.

The summer after my freshman year, my friends and I wanted a restaurant job at Short Sands. I was too young to work in a restaurant as a waitress, because they served liquor, and many of the other positions had already been filled, mostly by college students. Still, I wanted to be like the rest of the group, and soon there was an opening at the ice cream window at Spiller's Restaurant. I took orders from the restaurant side and a window on the street side, so anyone walking by could get an ice cream. The beach was across the street. I worked 2:00 P.M. to 9:30 P.M. There were two of us at the window, and we were very busy.

After work, my friends and I usually walked back to Long Sands. If it was bad weather, someone's parents picked us up. I had a day off from Spiller's every week, and lots of ice cream that summer!

* * *

My high school years were busy, and there were many changes in my life. My parents separated during my sophomore year, and that was hard. They had separated before for a while, but this time it was permanent. The Maine cottage was sold because my mother, who was still working in Dover, did not want to go there for the whole summer.

It was more difficult for Ellen than for me. I needed to watch Ellen, who was in grammar school. As I've mentioned, she was often sick. It was not until many years later, when Ellen visited an eye doctor, that she learned she was a brittle diabetic and started on insulin.

In high school I was also busy with my friends and with the work from my college prep classes, including Latin and chemistry. Once, in my chemistry class, our teacher left the room. We were supposed to wait for him to return before doing any experiments, but a few of the boys decided to mix some chemicals. There was a very strong odor that went through the hallways, so someone on the first floor pulled the fire alarm. The school evacuated and we all left in a hurry; our class decided to mix in with the other students so we would not be caught.

The police and fire departments responded. It was a cool fall day, and none of the students had their coats on. All the windows were opened, but we did not go back to the lab because it was time to go to the next class. Our lecture came later!

On weekends, girls who could borrow the family car got together, rode around to see new places, went out to eat, or attended parties, sleepovers, and football games. There was also a junior prom and a senior prom, and I went to both with my good friend Joe, whom I had known since kindergarten. The years went by, and I developed new friendships.

* * *

The summer between my junior and senior year, Aunt Rose suggested I work at the hospital as an aide to get a feel for hospital work. My mother said, "If you last, you might have a chance to become a nurse."

I had no problem getting a job. I started cleaning up after patients, washing beds when the patients left, cleaning bedpans, and doing odd chores. I knew the hospital well by the end of the summer.

I usually worked 7:00 A.M. to 3:00 P.M., five days a week. The hospital was old and had a tunnel to the nurses' quarters; at this time, it was used for administration offices. I delivered papers to administrators and met a lot of people. The staff knew I wanted to be a nurse and showed me different things, including a childbirth.

As a senior in high school, I had a decision to make. I still wanted to be a nurse, but where did I want to go to school? I had to apply, and would I be accepted? Many of my classmates were doing the same thing: trying to decide where to go for college. My aunt was a big help; she knew all the hospitals with nursing programs.

Nursing schools at the time offered three-year diploma programs, and after graduation students took state boards; if you passed, you had RN (Registered Nurse) after your name. Aunt Rose also knew about a new, four-year program that had started at Saint Anselm College in Manchester, New Hampshire. The program was not accredited yet since the first class had not yet graduated or taken state board exams, but both were set to occur in June. The students would graduate with a BSN (bachelor of science in nursing).

A four-year program was clearly where nursing education was headed. Aunt Rose was sure it would be accredited; she knew the nurses who had started the program, and she recommended Saint Anselm. I applied and was accepted, even receiving a small scholarship for my freshman year. I talked my father into paying for the rest. At my high school, a photo was taken of the seniors going on to college, which was an honor.

I spent that summer working at Wentworth Hospital as an aide. As fall approached, I was excited—a new adventure.

Chapter 2

College Days
1957–1961

In 1957, I started classes at Saint Anselm College, class of 1961. I was in the fifth class of nursing, which had twelve students; it was now accredited.

Saint Anselm was a male-only college, but they had started the nursing program in 1953. Since there were no dormitories for females on campus, many of the students lived at home, but those who lived quite a distance from campus were given rooms with Elliot Hospital student nurses. Saint Anselm students had the top floor of that dormitory. There were six from my class and we were each assigned a roommate; mine was Louise. Across the hall was a girl named Brenda Reid from Connecticut (the only one from out of state), and she also had a roommate.

The first day of school, during orientation week, upperclassmen brought the entire class, females included, downtown to Elm Street in Manchester. We were all given beanies to wear and did whatever the senior class wanted us to do.

Brenda was beside me, and one senior kept picking on her. I said, "That one kind of likes you; watch him." His name was Jay Meehan. I was right. He dated Brenda beginning our freshman year. They are married and have five children and thirteen grandchildren. I am the kids' adopted aunt.

Most of our freshman classes were liberal arts courses, but I was more interested in the nursing classes. The same was true for my roommate, Louise. Consequently, neither of us did much studying. She was older and had her own car. I knew nothing about Manchester, but we often explored the area together. I did okay in my nursing studies, but at the end of the year I had not done well overall and was given the option of going to summer school to make up a few classes.

I had to explain this to my mother and aunt. They said it was my decision. If I didn't go to summer school, I could get a job and forget nursing. I would need to save money for another school, and I might not be accepted.

I really wanted to become a nurse, so I told them, "I'm going to summer school."

At the time, my mother was working at the University of New Hampshire, so I registered there and spent the summer in school, meeting several other students in the same situation. We all learned a valuable lesson.

I returned to Saint Anselm in the fall with a new outlook. Four nursing students had dropped out, including my roommate and Brenda's roommate, so now Brenda and I became roommates. Brenda was still dating Jay, although he had graduated. We knew we had to graduate. Three years to go. Sophomore year, we lost two more students. By junior year, the nursing program had six left.

Our classes still included nursing and liberal arts classes. Our clinical time at the hospitals was increasing. Since we were not affiliated with one hospital, we traveled to different facilities. For example, medical and surgical clinical work was sometimes held at Elliot Hospital or the Veterans Hospital in Manchester. Obstetrics, nursery, and pediatrics work was held at the Elliot. For psychiatry work, we traveled to Concord Hospital in Concord, New Hampshire. Infectious disease clinical work occurred at a Veterans Hospital in Western Massachusetts, geriatrics clinical work was done in a New York City nursing home, and our visiting nurse experience took place in Worcester, Massachusetts. Life was interesting.

While in Worcester, we lived at the YWCA (Young Women's Christian Association). Brenda and I shared a room, and to save time in the morning, we shopped ahead for milk, orange juice, and donuts, which we stored on the windowsill. Once we started the day with our patients, we rarely had lunch. We ate our evening meals out.

The room was always cold, and one winter morning when we got up, both the milk and the orange juice were frozen solid, so we had no beverages with breakfast. I was so angry and cold, I made a beeline to the manager to complain about the cold room and our frozen food. The room remained cold. I found that visiting nursing was interesting, but I was glad to leave that place!

One weekend, I took three of my classmates to Dover to meet my mother. By that time, Ellen had graduated from high school and moved to California with her best friend, who had family there. Both girls had positions waiting for them. My sister stayed there for three years before returning to New Hampshire.

My mother was eager to meet my friends, because I had often spoken of them. Our group included Brenda (my roommate), Judy Charbonneau (who lived in Manchester and often invited us to her home), and Karlene Burns (another nursing student from Saint Anselm).

I borrowed my father's car, and on Friday after class, we left Manchester. No one checked the weather, but the roads were clear and Dover was only an hour's drive away. However, before I even left the West Side of Manchester, it started snowing, and it was really beginning to pile up. Someone suggested we should cancel our trip, but she was out-voted, and I kept driving. It was dark by the time we reached Raymond, which was about the halfway mark.

The roads had several inches of wet snow, and I could barely see a big truck coming right at us in the middle of the road. I pulled over to the side and ended up sliding down a little slope. The truck went by. We tried to move our car but had no luck; we were stuck.

We got back into the car and waited for help. No one drove by, and time passed. We were not prepared for this surprise Nor'easter, nor were the roads. I knew my mother would be a nervous wreck since we were due hours ago, and I thought, *"She must be calling the police by now."* Sure enough, she called the New Hampshire State Police and reported that four Saint Anselm students heading for Dover were missing.

They started checking the roads, and when we saw some light, two of us left the car and started waving our arms. The police found us and called the nearest public works department. A big truck came, and they pulled the car out. They gave me directions on the best way to go, and the police called my mother.

Once we made it to my house, we all camped out on the floor that night, talking about our adventure. My mother was happy she had a full house.

* * *

During my senior year, we still had six nursing students in our program. We had to finish our final exams, graduate, receive a BSN degree, then sit two days for the state board examination for our registered nurse certificate, the RN.

We were all anxious, and everyone had a plan for the future after graduation. I had a position lined up at Wentworth Hospital, Millie was going to graduate school, Julie had a position lined up in Manchester, and Karlene had a position lined up in a Manchester hospital. Judy was getting married to a Saint Anselm graduate, Jim

Lynch, and would work in Manchester for a while. Brenda would marry Jay the week after graduation. I was going to be one of her bridesmaids.

One day, as graduation loomed, I was sitting in a classroom studying for a final exam and talking to another student about the future. I had already spent a lot of time over the years at Wentworth Hospital, and I felt ready for something different. But what? I needed more nursing skills, I wanted to travel, and, of course, I needed to be paid. My nursing instructor overheard me. She suggested I consider the Air National Guard, of which she was a member. I asked a few questions.

Then she said, "What about the military?"

I said, "I know nothing about them."

I asked more questions, and she suggested that I call them. I didn't know how to reach them or who to contact. She told me to pick a branch and then call the recruiting station in Manchester. They could give me the number for the nurse recruiter.

I thought about it that night, and the next morning after my exam I called the Navy recruiter, who gave me the number in Boston for the nurse recruiter. Her name and title was Lieutenant Commander (LCDR) Roberta Perron, Nurse Corps, US Navy. I had lots of questions, and at the end of the call I asked her what made the Navy different from the Army and Air Force. She suggested that she visit my campus and bring the other two recruiters.

This was arranged, and when they arrived I had three recruiters to question. However, the minute I noticed the Navy uniform, I made my decision.

The Korean War was over, and there were no other wars going on then, so there were no hospital ships to serve on. Medical evacuations (medevacs) were limited, and there were no hospital field units either. Going into the military as a female was not expected of

College graduation: Father, Darby, Mother

College graduation: Aunt Peg, Aunt Rose,
Uncle Harry, Darby, Mother, Father

women at that time. As a new nurse I would be working in a state-side hospital for at least two years. I would be safe.

It was a three-year obligation. I talked my classmate Karlene into joining the Navy too. We could not apply until we graduated and had our RNs. However, once we took the RN exam, we could start our applications. I was ready to go.

I told my mother my plans. She was not happy, nor was the rest of my family. However, I reminded her that she had gone to Ireland when she was twenty-two, and she really could not say much to deter me.

Graduation finally arrived for the class of 1961, and my family traveled to Saint Anselm College to see it. My mother, father, Aunt Rose, Uncle Harry, and Aunt Peg came. Ellen was still in California. Photographs were taken, and I said lots of goodbyes to my other classmates. We were the fifth nursing class to graduate.

The week after graduation, I took my state board exams. I had borrowed my father's car again, and as soon as I finished my last exam, I drove to Connecticut for Brenda's wedding. Since I was a bridesmaid, I needed to be there Friday for the church rehearsal and the dinner. There was Friday evening traffic, but I made it. Just as I pulled into the driveway, the wedding party came out of the house and got into cars. Someone took my suitcase, and I joined them. Two Saint Anselm graduates and lots of alumni attended the wedding, which occurred on June 24. The wedding went off like a charm.

Chapter 3

Working at Wentworth Hospital
Fall 1961

I drove back to Dover Sunday afternoon, and on Monday morning I started my new job as a graduate nurse (GN) at Wentworth Hospital. I told my supervisor that I had applied for a commission in the Navy Nurse Corps and that I had to wait for the results of state boards and then process the application. I said that I expected it would be a little while.

In late August, Karlene and I learned we had passed our boards and were RNs. I called the recruiter, and we set a date in September for Karlene and me to complete our applications at Navy Recruiting and the Armed Forces Entrance and Examination Station (AFEES) Boston, near South Station. Karlene was still living in Manchester, but we arranged to go together. However, the day before we were scheduled to go, Karlene told me that she had changed her mind and didn't want to join. I didn't want to join alone, so I called the recruiter and told her that I was still interested but needed to reschedule our meeting. I added, "I do not have transportation to Boston," thinking that would be the end of it.

The recruiter, LCDR Perron, said, "I will have a car at your house at eight tomorrow morning to bring you to your appointments." Then she hung up. It was already quite late in the day, so I was doubtful that she'd be able to make these arrangements.

When my mother came home from work, I told her I was going into Boston for my physical and other paperwork the next day. I told her not to worry because the decision wasn't final; they would put everything together in a packet and send it to Washington, then decide if I would be accepted. I explained that they were going to send a car to take me to Boston and back. I think she prayed all night the car would not show.

The next morning, my mother went to work at 7:45. There was no Navy car in the driveway at 7:50; at 7:55, there was still no car. At that point I was nervous, so I thought I was home free. But at 8:00 A.M. I looked again, and a Navy car was parked in the driveway. I went to the Navy Nurse Recruiting Office in Boston and met my recruiter, LCDR Perron, in her dress blue uniform with all its gold braid.

She informed me what the day would be like, and she had a sailor assigned as my escort to take me to all my appointments. We started out, and as we went by the Army section, an Army man yelled to my escort, "I see you have a live one."

My escort said to the Army recruiter, "She's an RN."

The Army man yelled back to me, "Don't sign any papers; I can give you a better deal."

The escort replied, "She also has a nursing degree, a BSN."

The Army man walked over to me and said, "I'm serious; I can give you a better deal."

I replied, "I'm going Navy."

We moved on, and the rest of my day was busy with a physical, interviews, and so forth.

At 3:00 P.M., I was sitting in LCDR Perron's office waiting for a ride home. She came in and told me that everything was complete and she had been in touch with Washington. She had the authority to offer me a commission in the Navy Nurse Corps right now. She would need to have some papers typed up, and then I would take the oath in her office by the flag, with people from the office as witnesses. My next official step would be Newport, Rhode Island.

She said, "Would you like to do that now?"

I answered, "Yes."

She left and came back twenty minutes later with papers to sign and several witnesses. Then I stood by the flag and took my oath. Everyone congratulated me: I was now a new Ensign.

LCDR Perron drove me home. We stopped for dinner, and she told me what to expect.

When we got to my house and I was getting out of the car, I thought, *"My mother is going to kill me."* Fortunately, she accepted it better than I had expected.

The next day I went back to work at the Wentworth Hospital and told them I was now a nurse in the Navy but did not expect to leave for a while. I did not have a class assignment at Naval Schools Command in Newport for Nurse Corps orientation yet.

A few weeks later, I was scheduled for my orientation but I developed a kidney stone and missed it. I thought that was the end of the Navy, but a doctor at the hospital assured me I would be able to join the next class.

While I was home recuperating, I had an unexpected but pleasant visit from my friends Judy and Jim Lynch, who were on their way home after their honeymoon. We didn't know it then, but we would meet again a few years later when Jim was in the Navy and stationed in Florida.

I was reassigned to a new class, but the timetable meant that I would graduate right before Christmas, so I would need to leave for my Navy assignment (which was unknown) between the holidays. I did not want to do that and leave my mother alone, so I asked to join the first class after the holiday instead. The date was changed to the very end of January 1962. In the meantime, I continued to work at the hospital.

Chapter 4

Ensign: Navy Life Begins
Newport, Rhode Island, 1962

At the end of January 1962, my mother, Aunt Rose, and Uncle Harry brought me to Portsmouth, where I took a bus to Boston; I spent the night with Brenda and Jay and learned that Brenda was pregnant. The next morning, they put me on the bus to Providence, Rhode Island, and then I took another bus to Newport. I had one suitcase.

Once in Newport, I discovered there was another bus that would take me to the base. I noticed other men and women waiting for this bus. It turned out that there were several basic and specialty training schools on base, such as for the nurses, supply, and those being assigned on ships. We were all dropped off at different buildings along the way, and I got off the bus with several other women at our barracks.

There were two barracks for nurses, and we introduced ourselves. More nurses arrived throughout the afternoon, and later we were assigned a room and a roommate. We had bunkbeds, and I ended up with the top bunk. Next to that was a room with a desk and two chairs; the next room had bunkbeds, too. There was a large lounge area and a bathroom (now called the "head"), which had sinks, commodes, and showers.

There were about sixteen nurses in each barrack. After we met our instructors and were told what to expect, we all walked to the officers' dining hall for dinner. We had not learned how to march yet.

After we unpacked, we learned a little about each other. We were from all over the US, and the majority had one to two years of nursing experience. Our reasons for joining the Navy were varied. We would be there for eight weeks, and we would be introduced to the military, especially the Navy. Nursing would come when we reported to our new assignments, which we would learn during week seven. I wondered, "*Will this whole class finish this 'boot camp for nurses'? Will I make it?*" In fact, some dropped out.

At 6:00 A.M., the day started with "Reveille" over the PA system. We had to rush to the head, shower, and be in the dining room by 7:00 A.M. Classes began at 8:00 A.M., and we couldn't be late—demerits for that!

Now we had our schedule, and every minute planned. First was a trip to the uniform shop. We had a list for every item. Nurses' uniforms wouldn't come until the last week, when we had orders to a hospital, so we wore the traditional Navy blue uniform for the next eight weeks. After we received the blue uniforms, there was a trip to the tailor shop to see the seamstress; all of mine were shortened and taken in.

Two days later, we received our altered uniforms, and we lived in them. Dress blues, shirts, bridge coats (like peacoats but longer), hats: everything you could think of. We called our shoes "granny shoes." They had a medium heel and laces. We wore them every day, although we would not wear them after we graduated from our class! Later, some of the nurses had them bronzed and used them for bookends.

We learned everything about our uniforms, including how to wear them correctly and pass daily inspections. Our allowance for uniforms (around $300) didn't cover very much. The rest came from our pay. Our closets were full of uniforms and all our civilian clothes were packed away, but we were able to keep one civilian outfit on hand to use on weekends. We only had a couple of week-ends free during the eight weeks (and only for a few hours); most people used this time to go into Newport on liberty. Buses from base dropped us off in downtown Newport, and even though it was still very chilly, it was fun to walk around the cobblestoned streets, stroll past the waterfront, peer in tourist windows, and see some of the older homes and mansions. We also had a chance to visit the local restaurants.

We had to learn military time. Our classes were usually held from 8:00 A.M. to 4:00 P.M. or 4:30 P.M. (0800–1600 or 1630 in military time). Then it was on to the dining hall and dinner.

One of our first classes was learning to march, and then we marched wherever we went. We learned the president was our Commander-in-Chief. Then about the Defense Department. Next we learned the history of the Navy: rules and regulations; uniform code of military justice; customs and protocols; ship and airplane identification; military rank, rates, and uniforms. We learned about other military branches, so we could recognize their uniforms and ranks, and about different departments and what they do.

We were under the Bureau of Medicine and Surgery known as BUMED. The head of this agency, a Rear Admiral, is called the Surgeon General (SG). BUMED manages all health care for the Department of the Navy, including the Marine Corps and their families. It also trains and manages several corps (Medical Corps, Dental Corps, and the Nurse Corps). The head of the Nurse Corps Division is a Captain, called Director and is also located in Wash-ington. The division is responsible for all aspects of nursing: admin-istration (direction, personnel policy, military requirements) and recruiting (training, development, promotions, etc.). The current rank is Rear Admiral (upper half) and the title is Chief, Nurse Corps. We had study hours at night and tests.

A few nights we went to the Officers' Club, and then we went to the commanding officer's quarters (home) to learn that protocol. In between marching we also had physical fitness, and we all had to know how to swim. We swam indoors in a huge, unheated pool with cold water. Most of us knew how to swim already, but there were some women who did not. It was mandatory to be able to get across the pool. During the Korean War, a hospital ship had left San Francisco and sunk off the coast of California. A few Navy nurses on board had not known how to swim, and they had lost their lives. Consequently, now every nurse had to know how to swim.

In late February or March, the entire class went to sea for a day. Navy destroyers were going on an exercise; the planes from the Naval Air Station went out ahead and made a drop. It was a signal that the ships had to retrieve on the radar screen and report. There were five or six ships, and the class was divided among them. Each ship had a different area. It was a cold day, and the seas were rough.

We wore our winter uniforms and our bridge coats (winter coats). Some nurses were seasick. The ship's crew were in and out of the ship all day with their duties, and we watched. When we wanted to get warm, we went back inside to watch the radar screen. That was where the captain was, so we didn't talk much. It was a long day until all the ships completed their mission and we returned to port. We now had an idea of what it was like at sea, and we also knew what our future patients might be doing at sea.

* * *

Back in our barracks we learned how to stand "watch." We did it every night until graduation. Someone was on duty every two hours from 10:00 P.M. (2200 hours) till 6:00 A.M. (0600 hours). While standing watch, we had to be in uniform, and we were inspected before our watch started. The security watch area covered both barracks. At the end of our watch we had to make a report. The 10:00 P.M. (2200) to 12:00 A.M. (2400) watch was not bad as we were still up and in uniform. For the others, someone would wake us fifteen minutes before we had to report for watch. We scrambled to dress in uniform, then got undressed after our shift. The watch from 4:00 A.M. to 6:00 A.M. (0400–0600) was better, since after the watch we were already up and prepared for the day, ahead of the group.

Our meals were very good—in fact, too good. The stewards in training always asked the nurses if we wanted seconds, especially for desserts, which were delicious. How could we refuse? The men at our table wondered why we were getting seconds and they were not. We told them they had to smile.

However, it was not long until some of us started gaining weight and our uniforms became a little snug. Our instructors didn't know why. So, we were all called in and told to watch what we ate. We had to write down everything we ate and why. I swear this was the beginning of Weight Watchers. We all did it. I had to explain why I had so much ice cream and peanuts. I said that I did not like milk but needed calcium; the peanuts gave me protein to keep me awake during my watches. They did not like that answer, so I was soon back to my original weight.

Weeks went by; a few classmates dropped out. The rest of us adjusted to the routine and started to think about the future. My recruiter told me to wait before buying a car since I might want to fly to my duty station if I ended up being stationed on the West Coast.

It was now week seven and we would receive our orders. Where would I be assigned? Would I like it? Would I be on the East Coast or West Coast? Would I be working in a teaching hospital? Everyone was anxious. We all knew we could be assigned to places we did

Darby after graduation with her mother, Newport, RI

not want. The needs of the Navy came first. In each barrack, the nurses met and the envelopes with our orders were given out.

I opened my envelope and read Naval Hospital, Naval Air Station Pensacola, Florida. I was pleased. It was a mid-level teaching hospital outside New England, in a warm climate, on the Gulf Coast. Perfect. I looked around; there were lots of tears and hugs. I asked, "Is anyone going to Pensacola?" No one else was. I wanted company.

I walked over to the other barracks and yelled, "Anyone going to Pensacola?" Two hands went up—Laurie and Carolyn. Great! We started to make plans. We decided that when we were allowed to move out of the Bachelor Officers Quarters (BOQ), we would pool our money and rent a house.

We had to let the chief nurse in Pensacola, a Navy captain, know the exact date and time we were reporting for duty. Laurie came from Rochester, New York; Carolyn was from outside Richmond, Virginia. They both had cars and they had each worked as a nurse for a year before joining the Navy. Laurie suggested I fly to her home; then we could drive to Florida together. She wanted company, and we could sightsee along the way. I happily agreed.

Soon it was graduation. Several of the classes at Naval School Command had Pass in Review. This is a longstanding military tradition that began as a way for a newly assigned commander to inspect the troops. Visiting officers and guest speakers are also invited to review the troops. My mother, Aunt Rose, and Uncle Harry came to Newport to watch. After the ceremonies, I went back to New Hampshire with them for a few days of leave.

A little history: The Army Nurse Corps, which was first, was established in 1901; the Navy Nurse Corps was officially established in 1908, though nurses had been caring for sailors on ships before that. The Navy Nurse Corps is smaller and provides medical care for the Marine Corps. The number of nurses varies according to the end strength of the Navy; at one point there were 2,500. The Air Force Nurse Corps was established after WWII. The rank structure names for the Navy and the Coast Guard are the same. The Army, Marine Corps, and Air Force are similar but different from the sea services. There is usually some confusion with ranks or rates between the seagoing services and the other branches. The military ranks appear in the charts at the end of this book on pages 288 and 289.

Chapter 5

Naval Hospital Pensacola, Florida
April 1962–February 1964

After my leave, I flew to Rochester and met Laurie. We stayed at her parents' house and left early the next day. We stopped to see her sister in Kentucky, and then we drove through the Blue Hills in Kentucky and down to Pensacola, pausing along the way to sightsee. It was April, and it was a beautiful drive. Laurie had a small red car and did all the driving, even though I offered to help. It was a fun trip. Two Navy ensigns off to save the world!

We arrived in Pensacola a day later than planned, and when we reported to the BOQ, we found out that one of our rooms had been given away. So, we were roommates for a while. Carolyn had reported in two days before us and knew a little of the place.

Our new home was a room in a large brick building with an officers' mess for three meals, although we would be at the hospital for many. It housed over one hundred men. The next day Laurie and I reported for duty, and then the orientation began for the three ensigns.

The next five weeks were very busy as we learned about Navy medicine, including duties of Navy nurses and all the paperwork. It also included supervision of the corpsmen and ward routines. After work we headed to the Officers' Club, getting more education on the Navy and the area we were in. I reminded the others that I needed to buy a car, but since we would be on base for a couple of months, I was told I did not have to rush.

At the end of the fifth week, surprise! We had five days to move out of the BOQ, because a large number of student aviators were arriving and would be housed together. We started looking for a house and found one not far from the base, with three bedrooms and two baths. We signed the lease and went back to the BOQ to move our things. A senior ensign named Irene asked if she could join us since she also had to move.

We said yes—more money for us—but she wanted her own room. Since Laurie and I were already roommates, we said we would continue.

We all knew we would be working different shifts and different places in the hospital. I looked at my schedule right after we moved and found I was scheduled to work the 3:00 p.m. to 11:00 p.m. shift in three days, and none of my housemates were on that shift. No ride to the hospital. Panic! One of the nurses offered to take me to a car dealership.

On the way, she asked which dealership I wanted to go to. I said I would buy a Volkswagen Beetle. As we drove onto the car lot, there it was, an aqua bug. I went to look at it, and as I was walking around the car, a salesman came over and asked if I would like to drive it.

I said, "No, I want to buy it, but I need it in two and a half days. If you can't do it, I don't want the car."

He asked, "How are you going to pay for it?"

"I'm an Ensign in the Navy," I said, "and I was told if I join the Navy Federal Credit Union for $5.00, they will give me a loan. I am in for three years and I can get a loan for three."

He asked if I had any other loans. I didn't, so he said we should get going on the paperwork. I signed some papers and said I would be back in a few days.

When I returned to the dealership, I was two hours late because I had not been able to get a ride on time. It was after 1:00 P.M., and I needed to report for duty at 2:45 P.M. I started signing papers. Lots of them. No time to really read them, and this was my first car.

At last the salesman said, "You've signed everything. The car is yours."

We walked quickly out to the car because at that point I was in danger of being late for work. When we got to the car, he gave me my keys and opened the door. I sat in the car and put the window down. I went to put the keys in the ignition, looked down, and froze. Maybe it was shock. I stared out the window like a statue.

The salesman put his head in the window and asked, "Is there a problem?"

I did not know what to say, so I stepped out of the car. He was quite tall, so I had to look up to speak to him.

I said, "This car has a standard shift. I thought all new cars were automatic."

He didn't say anything.

I said, "This car is a standard shift, and I don't know how to drive it."

He looked at me and said, "You bought a car and you don't know how to drive it?"

I said, "Yes, sir."

He was still looking at me, so I asked, "Would you show me how to drive it?"

"You really don't know how to drive this?" he asked.

"NO!" I said.

I was not going anywhere, so he got in the car and tried to teach me. All I could think about was how to get rid of this car. I had been in many cars with a standard shift, but I had never paid attention. I had learned to drive on an automatic.

When I took my turn, the car had constant seizures: I would stall it, flood it, grind the gears, and come very close to hitting other cars. The car salesman had one hand on the dash and another on the ceiling. Around and around we went. It was now 5:00 P.M., and at one of my frequent stops, he clearly wanted me to leave. He told me how wonderfully I was doing and said, "You're all set to go!" He was not telling the truth.

The roads were filled with 5:00 P.M. traffic, and after thirty minutes I made it out to the main road and started my trip to the base. At every stoplight, stop sign, and slowed traffic I stalled, and I was forever grinding the gears. At one of my stops, I put my nurse's cap on. (I was already in my nurse's uniform.) As I approached the main gate, the Marine saluted me and I returned the salute, but he didn't let me pass onto the base. He just kept walking back and forth.

I asked him if there was a problem.

He said, "You don't have a base sticker, and I cannot let you continue."

When I pressed him further, he explained that to get one I had to put my car in a lot outside the base, where the cars that were not allowed on base were parked. This included the cars with too many speeding tickets, ones that did not pass inspection, cars with no insurance, and so forth. My new car! How could I do that?

Then he said I would need to walk across the road to the Pass and Tag Building to apply for the sticker.

There were several more problems with this plan. First of all, I couldn't back up with a big line of cars behind me, so the Marine said he would stop the traffic coming off base so I could make a U-turn. I tried that, but it tied up traffic for some time. Both ways. Getting around the security island and backing up was a big problem.

I eventually made it to the office, but it was near closing time. No sticker. I needed to register the car and have it inspected and insured, and I did not have the title. Another trip to the dealership! I had all the forms, though, so I thought the Marine might let me go through.

I walked back to the security island and asked the Marine.

He said, "No, but I know all about you."

I looked at him and realized he was a different Marine; the other one had left. I asked about bus service to the hospital, but I had just missed it. It would be several hours before I would make it to the hospital.

I commented on how late I was for work, and he informed me that I was UA (Unauthorized Absence). I just looked at him. Then he went on. According to him, I was AWOL (Absence Without Leave) and could be court martialed.

I'm sure I turned white like my uniform. Five weeks at my duty station! And a court martial?

He suggested I go right back to the building, which was closing in five minutes, and call the hospital.

I called the hospital and talked to the supervisor, who assured me I was not going to be court martialed. She sent a Navy car to pick me up. The Navy chief she sent for this task never said a word. I think he was laughing at me as I complained about the dealership and the salesman. He seemed to be biting his lip as he looked straight ahead.

Then I started to worry about how I was going to get back to my car later on to drive home. I did not know where the car lights were or how much gas I had. I knew my address but realized that I wasn't even sure how to get there, and I could not call my housemates because we had no phone. (The phone company in Pensacola would not give a phone to four single women; we needed a male to countersign for the bill and we did not know anyone who would do that. Eventually the Navy had to help and we got a phone.)

It was after 8:00 P.M. when I finally arrived at the hospital. I started looking for the supervisor and remembered that I had heard that two other nurses, ensigns, also lived in our area. I had not met them but hoped one might be on duty so I could get a ride home. I was lucky; the supervisor let me leave with the ensign. The next morning, I returned to the base early with a roommate, found my car, and worked on getting my base sticker.

Darby and first car (the bug), Pensacola, Florida

Later that afternoon, a young male ensign asked if I was Ensign Reynolds and said he had been told I needed help with my car. He was offering to teach me how to drive. I declined his offer, but later the same thing happened: a second ensign also offered. I did not know who these two men were.

I told them, "Driving is a piece of cake." Then I asked the second ensign why he had come to me. It turned out that the chief who had picked me up the night before was sending them to me.

(This continued for almost a year.)

When the third ensign showed, I asked if he had a hammer and a screwdriver. I told him we had a few things at our house that we needed a little help with. He said he could do it and asked to bring a friend. I said, "Sure."

Soon our house became a meeting place for other nurses and young male officers, ensigns, and lieutenant junior grades (LTjgs). There was usually a group around and lots of discussions. Work was interesting—a challenge at times, but rewarding. On days off we explored the area. I never did the driving; no one wanted to get into my car. (I wonder why?) Instead, I helped pay for gas.

* * *

About four months later I was assigned to the 3:00 P.M. to 11:00 P.M. shift and had two wards: orthopedic and surgical. I was the only nurse for both, and there were two corpsmen on each ward, with sixty patients. These were pre- and post-operative patients, and a few in rehab (rehabilitation). Both wards were busy, and I was frequently going between them. The supervisor was busy in the dependent area.

Right after dinner, I received an eighteen-year-old patient from the OR/RR (operating room/recovery room) who had just had his appendix removed, nothing too unusual. I put him right in front of the nurse's station to observe him. (There were no Intensive Care Units—ICUs—then.) The ward was a long room with twelve patients on each side. There was another room next to this with twelve more patients. After an hour I noticed a change in him, and as protocol, I notified the supervisor. I spoke to the intern twice; he ordered lab work but never came to check the patient, so I asked the nurses to check for the resident in all the watch rooms.

We had a lot of difficulty finding the resident doctor; he was not answering phone calls. The search was on.

Eventually he was found, and I spoke with him on the phone. I reported the condition of the patient, noting how much the patient had deteriorated. I had previously checked the doctor's operating notes, and there was no drain. I had to put abdominal dressings on to absorb the fluid. Where was it from?

The resident said, "If the intern didn't feel it was necessary to come check the patient, I am not going to."

I said, "I don't think the patient will make it to the morning. His vital signs are changing."

Since a corpsman needed help, I hung up, and the corpsman standing next to me asked, "Now what?"

I told him I was calling Captain G., Chief of Surgery, who was at home.

The corpsman said, "You can't do that; only the doctors can call."

I had difficulty getting the chief of surgery's number from the front desk. They did not want to release it. I finally did get it, called him, and gave a report on the patient, explaining that the resident would not come to see the patient. I told him I expected the patient to be dead by morning.

I also said, "When the patient dies, the resident had better not say he would have come to check the patient if only I had called." (I had made entries in the nursing notes every time I had called the doctors.)

He never said a word. He just listened. Finally, I said the corpsman needed help and hung up the phone.

It was now 10:30 P.M., and the night crew would be arriving. I asked the corpsman to bring the dressing cart because I needed to change the portion of the patient's dressing that I had added. I knew something was not right. This time, I was able to lift some of the original dressing because it was loose, and I finally identified the problem. The patient had eviscerated, which means his incision had split open. I could see part of his intestines, and he was losing valuable body fluids.

I thought, *"He will be dead by morning. Who do I call now? The commanding officer (CO) of the hospital?"*

I put the dressing over the incision, stood up, and felt someone behind me, a breath on my neck. I thought it was the night nurse, but when I stood and turned my head, I realized that it was the chief of surgery.

"Would you like some gloves?" I asked, and I moved so he could take my place. He moved in, looked at the situation, and told the corpsman to take the foot of the bed. He told me to call the OR. He took the head of the bed, and they moved it to the OR.

After I signed off on the patient's chart and the corpsman brought it to the OR, I made rounds and double-checked other patients' dressings.

One patient asked, "Is the kid going to make it?"

I told him, "He's in good hands. The chief of surgery is with him, but if you're a praying person, you might say a prayer."

I then realized that the resident and intern did not know their patient was in the OR, so I sent a corpsman to tell both of them that Captain G. was with their patient. I stayed at the hospital until 5:00 A.M., helping and hoping to get word on the patient's condition. Eventually I went home, where my roommate, Laurie, was getting ready for work. She worked in the operating room, and I told her what had happened. I had the day off and asked if she could call me. I stayed by the phone all day, but as it turned out, she did not get the chance.

She did not arrive home till after 5:00 P.M. My first question was, "Is he still alive?"

She said only one word: "Critical."

I asked what had happened, and she said, "I can't talk about it. The whole department is not supposed to talk about it. There were closed-door meetings all day, and a couple of times I heard your name."

"Wonderful," I thought, in dismay. *"Maybe I should think of leaving the Navy since I broke a lot of rules."*

I didn't sleep that night and wondered why the chief nurse didn't call me.

The next day I reported for duty. I received a very cool reception from the charge nurse. I could see the patient in front of the nurse's station behind closed curtains. I had hoped I might be assigned to him. The charge nurse, a lieutenant, assigned me to the end of the ward. She was a good friend of the resident. I noticed the intern and resident were not there and that the ward medical officer had returned. I later found out that the intern and resident had left the hospital; I never discovered exactly what happened.

After a few days, I started getting positive news about the patient from the corpsmen: "The weather improved up north," "A few clouds came in but are expected to move on," and so forth. The patient soon improved and started walking.

I was moved to another ward, but after several weeks I returned to the surgical ward. The chief of surgery, Captain G., asked me to go on teaching rounds with the new team, an intern and a resident. It was interesting. I was asked to assist Captain G. in our treatment room on some procedures. Next, he asked if I would like to learn how to remove sutures.

Later on, there was a plane accident on base, and we had many patients. The ER was full, so the treatment room was used, and a patient required sutures. Captain G. asked if I wanted to learn how. I said yes.

The patient was wide awake, so I told him it would be okay; it would just be like I was sewing a hem on my skirt. The surgeon told him the incision area would be numbed, so I learned how that was done. Later the patient was admitted, and I overheard him tell another patient that I was the nurse who "sewed him up like doing her skirt." Things got back to normal on the ward.

* * *

My sister, Ellen, returned from California and decided to come to Florida to see me before starting her new job. It was October, during the Cuban Missile Crisis. I was working on a surgical ward, and we had been placed on alert. There were several staff from the hospital—doctors, nurses, hospital corpsmen, and others—who had their bags packed and were ready to leave when the call came. This team was restricted to the hospital on standby. If the missiles were deployed and hit the United States, we would be among the first to care for casualties. It was a wait-and-see situation.

Because I was so occupied at the hospital, my housemates had to entertain Ellen. My boyfriend, Ray, who was in the Navy, also showed her the area. Ray was in the Navy flight program to become an aviator. We had been dating for a few months.

The base was supposed to have an air show with the Blue Angels, but that was cancelled. However, people could go and look at the planes, and I was given a short time to see Ellen once the crisis was over.

* * *

The hospital had quarterly inspections by the commanding officer, and I checked the schedule because our ward was on the list.

I found my name and another ensign's name as being marked for duty, but neither of us had been involved with this type of inspection. I let the supervisor know, and she said she would check it out with the front office. They confirmed that the schedule would remain. We started preparing the ward: everything cleaned from top to bottom, records and medications checked, and all ambulatory patients involved. I lost the coin flip with the other nurse, so I led the inspection.

It was scheduled to start on Friday at 10:00 A.M. On Thursday, I stayed late and checked the ward. I knew all the patients and was confident that I would be able to tell the commanding officer their names, diagnoses, and status. The next morning, I went in a little early, as this was a working inspection and we had several patients going for surgery. The ward looked great. The patients had morning care, beds were made, and ambulatory patients were asked to sit by their beds. There was a piece of tape across the head door that said to use the one down the hall until after inspection. I thought it was a good idea.

Most of the inspection went very well. Then there was just one last area for the commanding officer to check before we passed: the head. I went to open the door to the head but could not; I tried twice. The inspection team was waiting. On the third try, the door opened a little. I looked in and all I could see were paper towels scrunched up into balls. The entire head was covered up to sink level. They looked at me for an answer. I was speechless. I could not think of anything. We had failed the inspection!

I was waiting for the commanding officer to say something. Then I thought, *"He is trying not to laugh."*

He turned to the chief nurse and told her to take care of this matter—meaning me and the other ensign, who was in tears.

I was furious. Who did this, and how?

My chief nurse turned to both of us and said, "I will see you immediately after inspection. We have one more ward to inspect."

After the team left, I turned to the senior corpsman for an answer. He explained that he had not warned me about the head because a chief petty officer had threatened to make trouble for him if he told me.

I knew exactly which patient he was talking about. That chief petty officer and one of his friends, a first-class petty officer from a different department on base, were a constant problem for the nursing staff. They had been patients on the ward a long time and were nearly recovered. Frequently they would sneak out at lights out, go to the Chief's Club for a beer, and return before headcount, at 11:00 P.M. Sometimes they would put pajamas on early and say how tired they were or make up a phony bed and leave. The next morning, the charge nurse would give them chores to do, and now they had seized this chance to get even.

I asked the corpsman how the chief petty officer and his friend had done it. Apparently, they had asked all the enlisted men in the hospital to make up the paper balls and deliver them after visiting hours the night before.

I went down to their beds to talk to them. They sat there with big smiles and asked how the inspection had gone. Of course they knew—they had planned it.

The other nurse and I went down for our lecture on leadership. She was in tears, but I started to laugh as I thought of all these men carrying containers of paper balls.

Then the chief nurse asked me if I thought this was a laughing matter. I said no. As we left the office, we were informed that the commanding officer would give the ward another chance after lunch.

I kept thinking there had to be a way to get back at those two men. It was almost noon and they were headed for the dining room, along with the rest of the ambulatory patients. We met, and they both had big smiles again and asked how our meeting had gone with the chief nurse.

With a big smile I said, "Great." I added, "The commanding officer is giving us another chance and coming back after lunch."

Their smiles disappeared. I told them that if we did not pass, I was going to do everything in my power to make sure that their liberty would be cancelled. Their liberty was from 4:00 P.M. Friday to 9:00 P.M. Sunday, and then on Monday at 8:00 a.m. they would be discharged from the hospital. I also told them that I had weekend duty and would make sure they were kept busy with all the assignments I had lined up; I also mentioned that their commanding officers might like to know about their trick in the hospital.

Before they replied, the chief petty officer yelled out, "NO one leaves the ward. We are being inspected after lunch, and we *will* pass this inspection."

All the men leaving for lunch turned around. Bed patients all received their trays, but the rest of the patients and staff went without. They could go to the snack bar later, but even so the patients were not happy with the chief and first-class petty officers. The commanding officer and part of the team returned at 2:00 P.M., looked at the ward, and inspected the head. We passed. At least it was not a failure. Another lesson learned.

* * *

All was going well. I would occasionally hear from my former classmate, Karlene, who wanted to see how I was doing and whether I still liked the Navy. Then she called me and told me she had decided to join the Navy. She spoke to our recruiter and told her she would join, but only if she had orders to Pensacola. She wanted to know if she could move into our house. My roommates were fine with the idea, so Karlene joined the Navy, went to Newport, and ended up in our house. Now we had five ensigns. The yard frequently looked like a car lot, with our cars and those of our friends.

Chapter 6

Engagement and Hospital Work
December 1962

My boyfriend, Ray, surprised me. He told me that friends were getting engaged and we would meet them at the Officers' Club to celebrate; he asked me to dress up. My roommates knew what he was up to and helped me dress. Ray and I went into the bar, sat in a booth, and waited for the other couple. I did not drink often but ordered a fruity drink with the fruit on a stick.

The waiter brought the drink, and I started moving the fruit around. Ray asked me if the drink was okay. The waiter, who was watching nearby, also asked, "Is the drink okay?"

I said the drink was fine, but the waiter suddenly picked it up and said he would refresh it. A few minutes later, he came back with another drink.

The diamond dropped from the first stick of fruit into the glass. I had not seen it, and before l lost the ring a second time in the glass, Ray proposed. I am not sure what would have happened if I had swallowed the ring!

The other couple was waiting, and we celebrated together. Later, I called my mother; my sister had already met Ray during her visit. Ray, who was from the Northwest, let his parents know. No date was set because we both had time owed to the Navy, and I could not be married and remain on duty.

* * *

I continued learning about the Navy. There was no housekeeping staff at the hospital, and the corpsmen did the cleaning after patient care was completed. One day, they buffed the ward floor. It had been washed and the new wax was down. A few of the corpsmen were in a heated discussion about whose turn it was to do it. They kept going back and forth. No one wanted to do the buffing, and they said it was hard to do. I saw the buffer. It was a big commercial one and covered a lot of territory.

It looked easy to me, a big dish with handles, so I said, "I'm going to try it."

They all protested, but I insisted.

One of the patients said, "Get set with your hands on the handles. Then I'll plug it in." That way, I would not have to move my hands.

They plugged it in, and the buffer took off. I ran behind it, trying to catch up. It hit the beds, turned around, and went after me and my shoes. To get away, I jumped on the buffer and was immediately spinning all over the ward, hanging on for dear life. The patients were laughing at me, and I didn't dare get off.

Suddenly, it was quiet. The patients looked at the door, where the chief nurse, Captain Bulshefski, was looking at me. Someone unplugged the buffer and I stepped down. I was so dizzy, I had a difficult time walking to her.

She asked what I was doing, and I told her. She said, "You could probably find something better to do." Then she asked me to stop by her office before leaving. Another visit to the chief nurse's office.

* * *

As the year progressed, I moved through most of the wards, with different specialties. One was SOQ, known as Sick Officers

Quarters. It was a busy ward, and it used a different setup. After spending a few weeks there, I was called back to duty very early one morning. Several other nurses had also been called and were present.

The supervisor had done a narcotic count and discovered that, in a small bottle of alcohol, 60cc of liquor was missing. (Though alcohol was not a narcotic, it was recorded with the narcotics.) The liquor was sometimes dispersed to very senior officers before their evening meal, ordered by the physician. No one was going home until we found out what had happened to it.

We searched all the records. It was already 3:00 A.M. and I thought, *"There are charts missing; they have to be in Medical Records."* However, that department didn't open till 8:00 A.M.

I told the supervisor about my idea and said I would stay since I lived the closest; I suggested that she let the others go home. She agreed, and I found the missing alcohol. It was a good lesson for us about documentation. We all needed to ensure it was recorded in the log and nursing notes.

Chapter 7

Naval Hospital Camp Lejeune
North Carolina, 1963

After I spent some time on leave in New Hampshire, my fiancé's parents flew down to Florida to meet me. We all had an enjoyable visit, but the hospital was very busy and I was not able to take the extra time off.

One day in early spring, I was notified that I needed to pack my suitcase. I was being sent to the Naval Hospital Camp Lejeune, North Carolina. There was an influenza epidemic, and two nurses were being sent to help. (There were no flu shots at that time.) I would leave in the morning and travel with a lieutenant commander. We would be there a month.

My roommates helped me pack, and I said goodbye to my fiancé. Once there, we reported to the chief nurse, a captain. The lieutenant commander had the night off, and I had to report for duty.

Since the nurses' quarters were full, we went to the BOQ. I changed and reported to the night supervisor, but I only had a sweater on, and it was cold. There was a little snow on the ground, but I had not taken my navy bridge coat because I had thought North Carolina would be warmer. She found an old nurse's cape, long navy blue with red lining, for me. It was nice and warm. She said I would be working out on the ramps and the nurse was waiting to be relieved.

She gave me a flashlight and pointed me in the direction, so I followed the path. It was dark, but finally I saw a light; the ensign was outside waiting. She gave me five sets of keys; each set had ten keys, most unmarked. There were five wards in World War II–era wooden buildings off the ramp.

The ensign nurse told me, "The lights above the door don't always work, nor does the buzzer to get in."

She said I might need to pound on the door, and someone would come. If not, I should go to the next ward and call.

"Let's go in," I said, "and you can give me a report on the patients."

She said, "I'm leaving; the corpsmen can do that." Then she left.

Each ward had between thirty and thirty-five patients. Most of them had the flu, but there was also pneumonia, hepatitis and infectious diseases, plus some measles and mumps. I had eight corpsmen for the five wards. I never saw the supervisor. She was very busy in the main building and dependent area. My hours were 7:00 P.M. to 7:00 A.M. on paper—in reality 6:00 P.M. to around 8:30 A.M. I was the only nurse on duty.

At midnight, the senior corpsman came and said they would be leaving for "mid rats." I had to stop and think: midnight rations. The cook would leave a hot meal for the enlisted staff; I did not get one. I checked to see if the wards had a little galley; they did, but no food. The patients couldn't even have a piece of toast. I had the corpsmen bring back food every night from the added galley so the patients could have a little snack. On some nights I would help them. Right before I left, the cook came to me to find out if I knew anything about all the missing food. I said that as far as I knew, there was no missing food. The Marines had the food. Every night we removed the food for the Marines.

It was a very busy month. I had two days off in the middle, very long hours, and little sleep. On average there were around 160 to 165 patients. They were not critical patients, but I had never had so many.

It was an eye opener, and I did learn a lot. However, I was very glad to return to Florida. Then I was reminded by my chief nurse that the Navy Medical Department provided medical care to the Marines and their families so I should not be so harsh. Even so, I had no plans to return to that base again.

Famous last words!

Chapter 8

Big Changes
November 1963

A month later, I was back in Pensacola. Karlene was settling in. My fiancé was not there; he had been sent to another base for more training. I was put on night duty. Afterwards, the nurses had long weekends (four days). A group went to New Orleans, and I joined them. We did lots of sightseeing and made plans to return. Schedules were getting interesting. I was back on my surgical ward and on night duty. I loved the beach, but the main Pensacola beach was ten miles away. We had a beach on base. Several of the night crew (nurses) would meet after work, have breakfast, change into our bathing suits, and go to that beach.

One day the helicopter pilots were out practicing their flying skills. They flew up and down the beach. Then one nurse noticed that they were watching us with binoculars, so we all waved to them.

A nurse who was dating a helicopter pilot said she was going to check into this. She did, and she learned that we could go up in the helicopters for a ride. We went out to the Air Station and found we needed to put on an orange flight suit and wear a helmet. When we went to put them on, they were filthy. We refused to put them on, which I think they expected. We complained so much they told us to take them home and wash them, which is what we did. Then we went back and they divided the group. That day we began our flying time, out over the Gulf and along the beaches. We did this often. Next we wanted to go up in the jets.

That was going to be a little more difficult. We needed to be checked out in the pressure chamber, swim across the training pool, and use the ejection seat. We started, but I had problems in the pressure chamber and kept losing oxygen. I tried a second time: same problem just a short time before completion. They decided I needed a different mask and had to order it. While I was waiting, I did the pool requirement. Unfortunately, duty intervened, and only one nurse went up in a jet.

The Navy was keeping us busy, and I saw less of my fiancé. His schedule and training often had him away, and I was on 3:00 P.M. to 11:00 P.M. shifts or nights. He was hoping for orders to the West Coast. If we married, I would need to break my commitment to the Navy. I didn't want to do that. At the end of October, I broke off our engagement.

* * *

More big changes were ahead. Our house in Pensacola was very crowded. We had reached the point when all ensigns would start to be promoted to lieutenant junior grade (LTjg). Earning more money meant we could move. However, a five-bedroom house would be very hard to find, so we decided to split up and move out. Laurie, Karlene, and I would live together; Carolyn and Irene would stay roommates. We had two months to let our landlord know, find a place, then move. The holidays were coming.

In the middle of November, I was again sitting in Captain Bulshefski's office, wondering what I had done wrong this time. She informed me she was sending me to the Army.

I thought, *"She sent me to the Marines, now it is the Army, maybe next will be the Air Force."*

I waited to hear what was coming next. I was being sent to Brook Army Medical Center, Fort Sam Houston, in San Antonio, Texas. There was a seat available for a nurse in their "Medical Management for Mass Casualties" course. What timing. We hadn't found a house, so I told my friends, "If you find us something while I'm gone, take it."

I left for Texas and arrived two days after President John F. Kennedy was assassinated. The base was in mourning, and I had to wear a black arm band. The course continued, and I was the only Navy nurse, although a few Army nurses were there for certain topics. After class, everything was closed or hours were limited: The Officers' Club, Commissary, Post Exchange, and so forth. There was no place I could visit, so in the evening, I read all the literature I received in class. I found the classes interesting, and I spent a little time in the Burn Unit, where a lot of research was going on. Then I attended an exercise for triage and setting up a field hospital.

* * *

I returned to Florida late one evening and learned that my friends had found a house but I would not be able to see it till the following afternoon. The next day, I reported to work, and my chief nurse asked how Texas had gone. I told her I thought I had learned a lot. Then she said that I would be receiving orders, but she could not tell me where I was being sent until the official orders came in. I was excited because I had put in for Spain, Italy, or Japan.

"I know you are leaving for New Hampshire in the morning for Christmas," she said. "I will notify you when the orders come in."

That night I told my friends I would probably receive orders but did not know when, so they might want to find another roommate.

They could move my things because I would not be back until late
December. Then, with everything packed up in boxes, I left for
New Hampshire.

Chapter 9

Orders to Vietnam
Christmas 1963

This was my first Christmas home since being on active duty. It was wonderful to see my family. I had ten days for leave, but it was really eight because two days were travel days. It was a very cold night, but inside all was warm and cheerful. The Christmas tree twinkled as my family and friends mingled. Around 8:00 P.M., I looked out the window and noticed the mail truck pulling up in front of our house.

"Could it be a late present?" I thought. But my roommates and I had agreed not to exchange presents.

The mailman walked up the drive, carrying an envelope. I went to the door and signed for it. It was a special delivery—for me. The envelope's return address was Naval Hospital Pensacola, Florida.

I carried the envelope into the living room and opened it. It was from my chief nurse. The letter inside read:

> *Dear LTJG Reynolds:*
> *Congratulations, you have orders to Saigon, Vietnam. Your official orders await your return. Enjoy the rest of the holiday with your family.*
> *Captain Veronica Bulshefski*

I stared at the letter. I had never heard of Vietnam. What happened to being sent to Spain, Italy, or Japan?

"What's so important that you're receiving a letter on Christmas Eve?" Mom asked.

"It's my new orders," I said.

"Where?"

I read the letter out loud.

"Where is Vietnam?" she asked.

"I have no idea."

"They're sending you someplace and you don't know where it is?" she asked, skeptically.

"Yes."

No one else in the room knew where Vietnam was either. My cousin Tom had heard of Vietnam but didn't know where it was.

"Get the encyclopedia," someone suggested. We found Saigon on a map of Vietnam. (See page xi.)

"It's across the Pacific Ocean," I said, thinking, *That's a long way from New Hampshire.*"

My mother glanced at the map and burst into tears, rushing out of the room. And that's how it went for the next two days; just looking at me caused tears and she had to leave the room.

"Why am I being sent to Vietnam, a place I've never heard of that has no hospital?" I wondered.

I couldn't wait to get back to Pensacola to learn more.

* * *

I left on December 27 for Pensacola. I had to be on duty the 28th. It was a long trip back with several plane changes. I reported to the hospital at 11:50 P.M. I needed to check in before midnight. The man on duty said, "You really cut that close."

I asked if he had my orders. He said they were in the personnel office and I couldn't get them until morning. Then he asked where I was going.

"Vietnam," I said.

"Oh, *you're* the one," he said. "The whole hospital is talking about you."

I was the only one going.

* * *

I left the hospital and drove to our new house. I had seen the house the night before I left for New Hampshire. My boxes were now in my new bedroom. I unpacked a few and got into bed; I had to work the 3:00 P.M. to 11:00 P.M. shift.

Laurie and Karlene were working the next morning, and I went to the hospital around 10:00 A.M. I needed to see those orders. When I arrived, everyone started asking me questions. I had no answers yet, but I learned a little before reaching the personnel office. A major coup had taken place in Vietnam in November; President Johnson was sending more troops to help the Vietnamese.

The big news for me was that the Navy had opened a one-hundred-bed hospital in Saigon in October 1963. Now I knew that there was a hospital in Saigon, and I was very anxious to see my orders.

My order stated my detachment date from Pensacola was the end of February. I would need to receive any immunizations required before going to Vietnam. I had leave time and then was scheduled to fly to Travis Air Force Base, near San Francisco, for my transportation to Saigon.

I called my mother to let her know I would be back home before I left. I emphasized that it was only a year assignment, hoping this would relieve her. Then I went on duty.

After New Year's, I received a letter from a commander who was the senior nurse at the hospital in Saigon. She told me all the things I would need and explained what to carry with me. I could also send a trunk. She advised me to bring Navy nurse uniforms, white nurses' shoes, white nylons, an alarm clock, a small lamp, and some extras. There was no place to buy American items near the hospital in Saigon because the nearest exchange was ten miles away and difficult to get to. Immunizations were a must with all the diseases I would be exposed to, plus the climate. I was responsible for my suitcase, and I could have only one to travel with.

There were seven Navy nurses, and I would share quarters with some. Lastly, she advised me to brush up on my operating room skills as I would share OR call with the nurses. I hated the OR; this was a BIG problem for me. I did not want to go, and I even put the word out for anyone interested. Maybe they could take my orders.

I went down to my chief nurse and showed her my letter. I told her I could not go and explained my aversion to the OR: One day, when I was a student nurse in the OR, I was standing by a wall with another student so we could watch a case. The surgeon who was operating started waving his arms around. He asked the assisting student nurse for an instrument, and while she was looking for it on the tray, the surgeon mistakenly cut a blood vessel and the patient began to bleed. The student handed him the instrument he had requested, but now he wanted another, so he threw it across the room, barely missing my eye.

Another surgeon had to finish the surgery. The original surgeon had a reputation for doing things like this. At that point, I decided I would never work in surgery.

I continued to tell my chief nurse that I thought I would be better suited to Spain or Italy, where I might not be needed in the OR. She continued reading the letter and looked at me with a smile.

"No," she said, "you are going to Vietnam. I will make sure you have some time here in the OR before you leave." That was not what I wanted to hear.

My roommate Laurie, who worked in the OR, gave me a crash course on procedures. I sat up at night and read the books, thinking, *"I'll never make it in the OR."*

The weeks were going by too fast; the news was out about fighting in Vietnam and wounded Americans. That meant the operating rooms were busy. I did not like that.

I needed to get those immunizations, so I went to the clinic. There was a large map of the world. I found where I was going and learned what I needed. There were several vaccinations required. I decided I would not do it on Friday but wait until Monday, because I had plans for the weekend and did not want to spoil them with any adverse reactions to the vaccines. Monday, I went back and found out that the entire supply of immunizations had been given to the Army, which had used up their own supply of immunizations because the troops going over to Vietnam needed them. They had forgotten me.

Now they had to order them. The immunizations arrived the day before I detached from the hospital, which meant I had to get a large number of shots at once. Otherwise, I would have to delay my detaching and end up with a shorter time at home, because there was a specific date that I needed to be at Travis AF Base in California. As I received the vaccines, I felt like a pin cushion and was not sure what would happen to me.

The next morning, I went to the personnel office for my orders. My car was packed. I had planned to sell my car, but no one wanted to buy it. I wonder why?

Some of my friends suggested that I stop by the cafeteria so they could come down for our last goodbye. The hospital staff came, too. My nursing supervisor came down and finally told me I needed to leave. It was 11:00 A.M., the lunch crowd would be coming in, and I needed to get started for New Hampshire. I had completed my first duty station and was on to my next assignment, Vietnam, with the recommendation of my Chief Nurse, Captain Veronica Bulshefski, Nurse Corps, USN, who later became Director of the Navy Nurse Corps 1966–1970.

Chapter 10

Brief Return to New Hampshire
February 1964

I left Pensacola with so many tears, I could hardly see where I was going. I made it off the base and said to myself, *"Turn off the tears and dry them; you have a long drive in this car."*

I still hated the "bug." I also thought, *"I hope I don't get lost too many times. I wonder how long it is going to take. Will I run into a Nor'easter?"*

Gradually I made progress to New York City, where I promptly got lost in Harlem. I did see a lot of New York City.

Finally, I was over the bridge. It was late when I made it to New Hampshire. I left the car in the driveway, thinking, *"I'll move it in the morning."*

My mother was waiting; she was glad to see me. The next morning, she woke me. She asked me to move my car, which was blocking the garage, so she could get out her own car and drive to her job at UNH in Durham.

When I went out to move the "bug," it wouldn't start. There was lots of snow, and the temperature was way below 0° Fahrenheit. My mother got a ride to work from a friend, and I called all the local garages for help. They were all very busy, but one agreed to help, and three hours later, a wrecker arrived.

I ran to put my boots and winter coat on. The mechanic was looking at the back end of my car. I told him I thought it was my battery and he should be looking at the front of the car. He looked at me and said, "Lady, I am looking at your battery now."

What a surprise! I never had gotten anything on the car checked. It's a wonder the car lasted two years and made it to New Hampshire. I felt like an idiot. I told him to take the car back to the garage and check it well, because I intended to sell it. The car went up on the wrecker, and I did not get it back until two days before leaving for Vietnam. I needed the car to do all my errands in a rush before leaving. What a headache!

Chapter 11

Travis Air Force Base
Fairfield, California, March 1964

Through a few more tears, I said goodbye to my family and took a cab to the bus station, where I caught the bus to Boston, a two-hour trip with stops. Then I boarded a flight to San Francisco, which took several more hours. Upon arrival, I took another bus to Travis Air Force Base. Between the waiting and that travel, that took another four hours. At the terminal I had to wait again because the sign said a staff member would appear every hour on the hour. I had my large suitcase, a white Samsonite with big black flowers that made it stand out. My roommates in Florida had helped me pick it out. No solid black bag for me. Although I could find this one easily, I could hardly carry it because of its weight (sixty pounds).

I also had a very large envelope with orders, pay record, health record, personnel file, and travel orders. I was dressed in my wool service dress blue uniform and high heels.

At that point, I was exhausted. I had not slept the previous night and had gotten little sleep for several days before leaving I was anxious about the trip and the new assignment.

On the hour, I handed over my orders to the young airman and was told to have a seat. He said they would let me know when there was a flight. He went through a door to an office in the back with my orders and then disappeared. I did not see anyone else until the next hour, when he reappeared, waited ten minutes, and then disappeared again. This continued throughout the day. No one else showed up for travel, although occasionally someone walked through the terminal.

As the day passed, I continued to be the only one sitting in the enormous terminal, which could have held more than several thousand people. I thought back to WWII and Korea and imagined how this place must have been filled with troops going to the Far East.

Whenever I wanted to use the restroom at the other end of the terminal. I had to carry my suitcase (no wheels) with me. I could not leave it standing by itself. I had everything I would need in that suitcase because my trunk, which was being sent by ship, might not arrive in Vietnam for a couple of months.

There was nothing to read. Instead, as I quickly learned, there were lots of wooden seats, a food machine with sandwiches (some of them oozing out green stuff), a soft drink machine, and a vending machine that had crackers. Coffee was warm water with powdered coffee and cream.

(For three days I lived on peanut butter crackers and Coke.)

At 7:00 P.M., I was told I could leave and was instructed to be back at 7:00 A.M. I grabbed my suitcase and walked to the transit BOQ. My room was on the second floor—no elevator and no one to help. I shared the bathroom with another officer, who had spent a good part of the night drinking. He locked me out of the bathroom, so I needed to dress in my uniform to go down to the desk to get someone to unlock the door. Another night without sleep. I kept telling myself, *"I will be gone today."*

The second day, around 5:00 P.M., about a hundred Army troops came in grouped in small numbers and went out the other door. After they left, I asked the young airman where they were going.

"Vietnam," he said.

I asked why I wasn't going with them. He didn't know and told me to go back and have a seat.

Since I didn't have anything to read, I decided to look in my envelope, which was taped and said, "Do Not Open." I planned to memorize the form numbers so that I'd know them when needed. Inside I found a message off the teletype requesting that they expedite my travel. They were short a nurse.

I had to wait for the airman to reappear, at which point I showed him the expedite order. He took it in back but returned and said they still had no transportation for me to take to Vietnam. That night I remained in my uniform because I expected a knock on my door any minute to announce that a plane was waiting for me.

I still had the same neighbor next door, and I was locked out of the bathroom again. I was in uniform and made the trip down to the desk to have someone unlock the door again. It was time to payback the neighbor, so this time I locked *him* out. He had to go for the key.

The next day, at 5:00 P.M., I learned they finally had a ride for me. I was instructed to take my suitcase and follow the line. I had to return to the BOQ to get my suitcase, because I had grown tired of carrying it back and forth. Once I was back in the terminal, I went out the door and saw about a hundred men in single file: Army troops with bags and rifles.

I followed the line down the tarmac to a large plane. When I was closer, I recognized it as Air Force C-130, a cargo plane with no windows. Six soldiers got in line behind me. We all went to the ramp at the rear of the plane and handed in our luggage. Then we went to the side and up the stairs. I was still in a skirt and heels. When I got to the top, I was told to take a seat.

I looked in and found that one side of the plane had very large wooden crates strapped in. The other side had rows of three wooden seats attached to the floor. The back of the wooden seats only came to my shoulder and lacked a head rest. All were facing the rear of the plane. Every third row, a light bulb was suspended on a wire. The plane was all metal and the floor had grooves. I had to be very careful that my heels did not get caught in the grooves, which would break them. That would be a serious problem.

I kept walking, looking for a seat. When I reached the ramp at the rear of the plane, I noticed a big net with all the bags, boxes, and my suitcase. Across was a bin with the rifles. There was an empty seat between two soldiers, and I decided to take that. I didn't want to get any closer to the ramp because those six seats were going to be very close to the net.

I asked the soldier on the end to move so I could get to the seat in the middle. He did not see me coming. When he finally stood up and saw me, he looked at my hat, looked down to my feet, and glanced back up. I had just been inspected by a young enlisted man, and he seemed to be in shock. He turned white—I thought he might faint. A female, officer and Navy, was going to be sitting next to him. I was the enemy. The other soldier did not look well either.

There was no place for my hat, orders, or purse. I put the orders behind my back, my hat between the soldier and myself, and my purse on the floor around my foot. Now the seatbelt. Where was the head? Back up toward the front. A curtain on a rod and between two crates. Behind the curtain was the head. No water for me.

It was a propeller-driven plane, and there was no intercom. Messages from the pilot were sent row by row to each person. I was in the tail. There was no food. There was no insulation, and it was very noisy. It was difficult for conversation, and with no lights except those hanging, it was on the dark side.

I kept thinking I was on the wrong plane. I asked both soldiers if this plane was going to Vietnam, and they said yes. Whenever I asked a question, they both snapped to attention. We finally left the ground. No one would speak to me, but if the pilot sent word down, they would relay that message. The pilot sent word as we went over the Golden Gate Bridge.

At least six hours later, we landed in Hawaii. Girls were giving out leis. The troops were told they had five-hour liberty. There was an engine problem, and parts were being sent in from the States. The men were in summer uniforms, but I was in my wool winter uniform and it was hot, so I decided to stay in the terminal, which had air conditioning. It turned out to be a nine-hour wait. When I went back on the plane, I took the aisle seat and let the two soldiers sit next to each other. That way, they could talk without me in the middle, and it gave me more room. I was the only female on this plane.

We flew back out over the Pacific, and after a short time the plane became very warm and humid. Then condensation started forming on the ceiling. These drops of water began to fall inside the plane, and everyone was getting wet all over: the top of our head, hair, eyes, nose, and uniform. Small water cups were passed out, and we were told to catch the water. Try to catch water from the ceiling in a paper cup! I quit. I kept thinking, *"Where is this water going? Is the plane going to sink?"*

Then my biggest problem began. In Florida, my uniform—along with my roommate's—had been packed in boxes filled with mothballs. I can assure you, no moth would see the light of day if it was near one of these boxes. New mothballs were added frequently. I had aired my uniform out on a windy day before leaving New Hampshire, but now the humidity in the plane was settling into the wool and producing strong fumes.

The new odor went through the entire plane, and all fingers pointed to me. The men kept yelling, "What is that awful smell?"

If I had been equipped with a parachute, I would have bailed out.

Several hours later, we made an unscheduled landing on Guam. We were out in the middle of nowhere. Nothing in sight except one small building. We went into the building and were told not to leave. We were behind schedule, and if someone walked away, that person would be left. The plane was moved a distance from the building, and men came in on trucks to work on the plane.

The building did not have enough seats, and there was only one very small bathroom. Windows looked at the runway. As usual, no one was speaking to me. I was still the enemy. Maybe it was the uniform.

Two hours went by. I was miserable; it was over 90 degrees, and my uniform still had the mothball smell. Now I had a new problem: edema and lots of it. My feet were so bad I could barely see my shoes. I put my hat on, left the building, and headed right to the plane—a walk.

My goal was to retrieve my suitcase so I could change into my summer uniform and flat shoes. Several of the troops had moved to the window to see what I was doing, and men from the plane were sent to try to stop me and bring me back to the building. I just ignored them and kept going.

I made it to the plane, and I told the men what I wanted. They said they could not take the net down. Everything would spread once the net was opened, and they had no way to lift it back up. They instructed me to go back to the building. Another walk with the sun beating down and perspiration dripping down my back. I was not a happy camper.

I approached the building and noticed that several of the troops were watching me. Once inside, a junior man asked me when we were leaving.

I said, "Soon."

Another one asked, "Why are you going to Vietnam?"

At this point, I was not sure myself, but I wanted to answer his question. More troops moved closer to listen.

"I am a Navy Nurse, and I am assigned to Navy Headquarters Support Activity, Vietnam, and will be at the Navy Station Hospital in Saigon," I said.

The room was very quiet; you could have heard a pin drop.

Then, suddenly, all of them moved up close, right in front of me, and they started asking questions: where was I from, where was my duty station located, and so forth. I started to answer their questions, explaining that I had been with the Army when I had attended the "Medical Management for Mass Casualties" course in Texas. I wondered what had caused this sudden change in their attitude toward me. Then I realized I had said the key word: *nurse.*

The next couple of hours went a lot faster. I had questions to ask also. Two of the soldiers were a little older. They had been in Vietnam before and were now returning after spending some time in the States to learn more about their new assignments. Both were going north of Saigon. One told me he was going to be in charge of Special Services, in a place called Nha Trang, Vietnam, about two hundred miles north of Saigon. They had a place where the troops could come for a break in the fighting, R&R (Rest & Relaxation).

He told me that if I ever made it up there I should go see him, and he would make sure that if I wanted to go water skiing, ride in a boat, or go into town to one of the restaurants, he would take care of it. He also told me that Nha Trang was where the Army 8th Field Hospital was located, and several Army nurses were stationed there. He didn't know anything about Saigon, but at least I was learning about the country.

The plane was finally ready, and we all went back on. I was exhausted. Days had gone by since I had left New Hampshire. I sat on my wooden seat but nearly fell off, trying to stretch my legs in the aisle. As I started to doze, I heard a lot of noise coming from the back. Whatever message was being passed along reached our row. The soldier next to me shook me and said, "Hurry up and get your seat belt on. Make it tight."

He had to help me with my seat belt; I was too slow. Then we dropped several hundred feet and hit the ground. The plane was still moving but the wing was up, and the big net was moving. Then we went the other way, and the crates began pulling on their straps. I knew that if the straps broke, we would be crushed.

Some of the rifles were loose, and anything not secure was moving. It was dark, because the lights had gone out. My ears were popping, and I had a hard time breathing. Had we crashed? Was this it?

Then we evened out. We were still moving, and the lights came back on.

"What happened?" I asked the soldier next to me.

"Snipers!" he said. We had needed to come in fast.

My next question was "Are we in Vietnam?" The answer was yes.

Meanwhile, there was a lot of shouting from behind us: "As soon as the pilot stops, everyone get out! Do not look for belongings!"

I was all for this. The men behind me were all moving quickly.

I stood up and fell into the seat. I tried again, and the same thing happened. I was scared and ready to panic but then realized my legs were numb because they had no circulation. I had to move somehow; the two soldiers next to me could not move with me in the way, and the six men in the two rows in front were also waiting for me to leave first.

This time I was prepared, so I held on to the top part of the seat in front as well as mine. Then I put my right hand under the straps across from me, and between dragging and pulling, I made it down the aisle. When I reached the door, a blast of heat hit me, and I thought I was in a furnace. The smell was awful: rotten eggs, sewer, and dead bodies. All I could think of was, *"Don't let me get sick here."*

How I went down the stairs remains a mystery to me. Once I was down on the ground, I had to hold the railing because my legs were ready to let me fall. The rest of the troops were out. The copilot was up at the top of the stairs, yelling, "We have to move the plane!"

Snipers were still active and close by. I really didn't care about the plane at this point. The terminal was off at a distance, and I could not walk. My choices were to crawl or be carried, and the eight soldiers near me were not moving either.

I did not want them to be killed. I bent my elbows, and two of them carried me to the terminal. As soon as we moved a little, the plane moved. A couple of times we stopped to look back, as the shots were close by and we wondered if the plane had been hit.

When we were closer to the terminal, I saw a sign above the door: "Welcome—Tan Son Nhut Airport, Saigon Vietnam." On both sides of the door, there were also plaques of the different military branches.

The rest of the troops were already in. A female was holding the door open. She was in a Navy summer uniform, and I thought, *"I hope she is not who I think she is."* But then I could see the insignia: Commander, Nurse Corps. She was my new senior nurse.

It's important to make a good impression when you meet your senior officer. But there I was—her new nurse, LTjg Reynolds—in my wrinkled, mothball-reeking uniform, looking like I came in on a big wave. My hair was everywhere because I was in the wind tunnel from the propeller. I was being carried by two Army men, and my feet as this point looked like I did not have shoes on. I could not take them off, I had so much edema.

The men and I made it to the door, and her first words to me were "What took you so long?"

I could not answer; where could I start?

More shots from the snipers. The men behind me asked her to move, as they needed to get inside. I was carried inside the terminal, and someone found me a chair to sit on plus another that I could use to elevate my legs. I had made it. What next?

Chapter 12

Arrival in Saigon, Vietnam
March 1964

For the next three hours I sat in the airport with my legs elevated. All the troops who were on the plane were also there, and we were ready to turn our orders in. This procedure is similar to customs checking into a foreign country with passports and visas. I waited for my yellow envelope to be returned to me. It had to be brought in from the plane.

The woman who had met me earlier at the door introduced herself as Commander Ann Richman and explained that she was the senior nurse. She said she had spent most of the day waiting for me and would sit in the orientation class with me.

As we waited for the orientation class on the dos and don'ts of life in Vietnam, we could still hear gunfire. Several of the men came over to me to say goodbye. They had their bags and rifles and were leaving. I asked about their orientation since I had expected them to be in my class, but they said there would be no orientation for them. They were needed for the fighting NOW.

I saw shock on a few faces. Some of these young men of eighteen and nineteen made a few jokes that they might meet me again in the hospital. Then I looked around the room. As they left with their bags and rifles, there was no more laughter. Would these young men ever return to the States alive? Reality hit me.

CDR Richman also revealed that she had been in Vietnam only a week. She had been rushed to the hospital for her orientation because the previous senior nurse had taken CDR Richman's plane back to the States. They never met in Saigon.

While we were at the airport, CDR Richman explained many things, and I learned the following:

- There were seven Navy nurses in Saigon, and we were separated for security. I would be living with three other lieutenants: Elaine King and Carleda Lorberg, who had been there since the hospital opened, and Eileen Walsh, who had arrived the month before me. I would be the youngest and the only LTjg (junior grade).

- We were general staff nurses, and we would be living in a hotel that had been named the Brinks in honor of a General Brinks. However, it was just called the Brink or the Brink BOQ. It had been taken over by the US Army, and it billeted almost two hundred mid-ranked Army officers. The four Navy nurses had a suite. We were the only women there.

- The commander lived in an apartment building six miles from the Brink. She lived with two other nurses: LCDR Tweedie Searcy, who was a nurse anesthetist; and LCDR Bobbi Hovis, who had been a Navy flight nurse in Korea. CDR Richman's duties were mostly administrative, but she assisted with all emergencies and at meal times when available.

- There was a bounty of 25,000 piasters ($150.00) for the capture of Navy nurses. For this reason, we should not wear our uniforms when off duty in Saigon, only civilian clothes.

- There were nine doctors and seventy-seven hospital corpsmen. They were also separated for security reasons.

- There were six or seven nurses from Thailand; they were under three-month contracts. At the end of their contracts, they usually went back to Thailand for two weeks, then returned to Saigon and renewed their contracts for another three months. Sometimes they did not return to Saigon, so new nurses from Thailand were hired.

- There were also several Vietnamese workers helping; this group included our drivers and cleaning people.

- There were only two military hospitals in Vietnam. The one-hundred-bed Navy hospital in Saigon opened in October 1963, and the one-hundred-bed Army hospital in Nha Trang opened in March 1963.

- All the other Navy nurses had flown over on Pan Am, not a cargo plane. They had been given good seats and meals. However, if I had not opened my yellow envelope and found the expedite paper, perhaps I eventually would have been picked up by Pan Am too. I will never know.

- After the orientation and before going to the hospital, I would spend the next two days at Navy Headquarters.

Since CDR Richman needed to get back to the hospital, we left the orientation a little early, but first she had to take me to my new quarters. A hospital sedan with a Vietnamese driver drove us to Saigon, ten miles from the airport.

My ride was a culture shock. I knew nothing about Saigon, and there was very little written about it. There were many different nationalities, clothes, languages, sights, sounds, and smells. Little children were toilet trained on the sidewalk. There were no diapers, and there were lots of people living in shacks and poverty. One sight I particularly recall was a man lying on a piece of cardboard with little pigs and chickens all around him. He was sleeping under a piece of metal.

I kept putting the window down to listen. The closer we were to Saigon, the more I started to see a few taller buildings; it looked more like a city. For transportation, people used cars, trucks, motorbikes, and scooters. There was a tank that had not been moved since the coup. It was mind-boggling. We went by the embassy, passed a zoo, and came into a street with fountains and flowers called Tu Do. We were getting closer.

* * *

My building, the Brink, had six stories. There with a cement wall around it, barbed wire on top, and Army guards.

The Brink BOQ, Saigon

When we arrived at the Brink, we drove in and left the car; the driver took my suitcase. We went up one flight of stairs, and the Commander knocked on the door.

Two women answered, and I was introduced to my new roommates, Elaine and Carleda. The other nurse, Eileen, was working at the hospital. The commander came in for a minute and then left for the hospital. The roommates had been waiting all day for me. It was around 5:00 P.M.

They had arranged a blind date for me and were planning to show me the city.

I wanted to get my shoes off, take a shower, and go to bed. I needed to unpack and get my uniform ready. I was leaving in the morning at 7:30 for Navy Headquarters, in Cholon, Vietnam.

I had a quick tour of the suite. Coming in the main door, the elevator (open grill) to the sixth floor was right in front of our door, and the stairs right next to our door went down to the ground floor. Once inside, there was a small area on both sides used for storage for all four nurses and a large living room with a small balcony in front just large enough to stand on. On both sides of the living room there was a short corridor with two bedrooms and a bathroom on each side.

My bedroom was the end room, and I shared the bath across from it. I had a small bed, no closets, hooks on the wall, a small chest, and a table.

I was told to expect to see little geckos, which looked like baby lizards, and I certainly did. They were all over the place. Oftentimes I would wake up in the morning and see them a foot away on the wall next to my bed, looking at me.

There was a door at the end of my bedroom; it led to a walkway on the back side of the building. The top part of the door was glass, and there was a drape that I kept closed. I put the table in front of the door. The alley below had a wall and barbed wire on top. On the other side were Vietnamese families.

Across the living room there was another corridor with two bedrooms for my other roommates, a bath for them to share, and a small kitchen for the maid, Mama-san, who did our laundry and kept her cleaning supplies there. She was an older Chinese woman who spoke no English. There was no cooking in the suite except for Mama-san and her own meals.

We took all our meals at the dining room on the sixth floor. The dining room was quite large, and when we went to eat, there was a very large jar with malaria pills on the counter, with a sign reminding everyone to take them. Malaria was a big problem. We had several patients with it. Three meals a day were served. There was also a small lounge.

The roof patio was a very active place where all the military officers and guests in the city could come, meet with friends, and feel safe. It was open every day and into the late evening. Alcohol and beer were available. We could see for miles, hear the mortars, and see the flares go up at night. Sometimes we could hear gunfire. I was told that if we ever had to evacuate quickly, we should go to the roof and a helicopter would remove us.

* * *

I ended up going out with my roommates that first night, but I don't remember very much because I was so exhausted. One thing I do remember was riding in a cyclo, even though in orientation I had just been told never to ride in one. A cyclo is a bicycle with a cab in front that passengers sit in, with the bicyclist sitting high up in back. At orientation they had explained that it was very easy to drop a bomb in the cab section. This had happened to a soldier, who managed to pick up the bomb and throw it back at the bomber, but the bomber had already left the cyclo. It was a dangerous way to travel, and we could be killed.

It was late by the time I came back, and there was a curfew. I finally made it to bed but then heard gunfire close by—two or three shots, then quiet for a short time, then shots again and again. I was afraid to move. Finally, it was quiet, and I fell asleep.

* * *

When my alarm went off, I put my summer blues on. I decided I'd better go for some breakfast before going to Navy Headquarters.

When I walked into the dining room, the host saw me and asked if I was the new nurse. I said "Yes." We spoke for a few minutes, and then he wanted to know where I would like to be seated. I glanced at the room, and everyone was looking at me. I said, "By the window." Now I had to walk through the dining room.

Later, some of the men came up and introduced themselves. I asked about the gunfire I'd heard in the early morning. It turned out that one of the men had had too much to drink and was practicing.

I asked what he was using as a target, and the answer was "Rats in the alley." Apparently, he did this often. The men also mentioned that a building across the street had a lot of bats. Then I remembered that I had been told to keep all doors closed.

* * *

After a quick stop in my room for my purse and papers, I was off to Navy Headquarters to learn about this new country. Again, there was so much information. One important item was how to make a phone call to the States. I had to place my name in a logbook a week before I wanted to make a call, then record the date and time of the call. If my scheduled changed, I could not make that call and would need to go back and reschedule it. Also, I had only five minutes to speak. It was a trunk line and was an "over and out." If there were problems in the line, it was our loss. I thought, *"Hopefully, my mother will talk quickly—otherwise the five minutes will be up and the person behind me will take his or her turn."* I decided that since I could lose so many minutes, it would be better to write.

I also learned that Headquarters was responsible for the Navy personnel in Vietnam and all the supplies that came by ship. There were many ships. I would find that I rarely went there, since the hospital was my work area and a distance from Headquarters.

* * *

On my third night, my trunk arrived. I was surprised to see it so soon. I got busy unpacking because I was scheduled to go to the hospital in the morning. I was anxious to see the hospital and start taking care of patients. It was late, and one of my roommates came to my room and said I should see what was happening outside our building. I was already dressed for bed but put a muumuu over my pajamas and went out onto the balcony.

The curfew had started, and all was quiet except a long military parade going right past our quarters. The parade contained all the heavy military equipment to be loaned to the South Vietnamese Army. The Vietnamese Army had been waiting months for these ships to arrive from the States filled with planes, jeeps, trucks, and so forth. First came the planes, lots of them. The wings on these planes were folded. Each plane was pulled by a jeep that was filled with ARVNs (Army of the Republic of Vietnam); another jeep followed each plane with troops for protection. Each piece of military equipment had the same VN (Vietnamese) military protection, so there were lots of ARVNs.

Our Army guards were watching also. All this equipment was going to the South Vietnamese military to help with their fighting. Some was headed for Bien Hoa, an Air Force Base ten miles from Saigon.

Elaine said, "I'm going to take a picture," and went for her camera. Carleda went next.

"If they believe this is important, I had better get mine," I thought. It was still in my trunk—a German camera given to me by my uncle—and I needed to put the film in. Off I went.

The three of us squished together on the tiny balcony. Elaine said, "Here comes the picture I want." Her camera flashed, followed by Carleda's and then mine.

Chaos immediately erupted because the Vietnamese Army saw the flashes and thought we were shooting at them.

They stopped the parade, and all the troops poured out of their vehicles. All the rifles were pointed at us.

"Don't shoot! It's the nurses!" our men shouted to the Vietnamese.

Then they yelled to us, "Don't move!"

This went on for some time. We did not move. All it would have taken was one shot and we would have been killed.

There was so much shouting that some of the men in the BOQ came out. One spoke Vietnamese, and he told the soldiers we were taking pictures with flashes. Then the Vietnamese wanted our cameras.

One of our guards said he was coming up for our cameras. The three of us dashed inside.

Elaine said, "They're not getting my camera" and went straight to her bedroom. I decided they were not getting mine, either, but

I agreed to give them my film, and Carleda did the same. I had nothing else on my film and thought I could get a copy of Elaine's picture. Later we learned it had not come out. We were nearly killed for nothing.

I did not sleep well that night, thinking how close I had been to being killed: first my plane ride, then the gunfire outside my door.

* * *

The next morning, I finally prepared to go to the hospital. I dressed in my white nurse's uniform and waited for the Navy sedan, which would pick me up at 9:00 A.M., giving some of the staff a start on morning routines (bed baths, linens changed, dressings changed).

All of the nurses, including the Thai nurses, were transported back and forth from their quarters to the hospital in a hospital car. We had Vietnamese drivers, and unless we were sharing a ride, we were alone with the driver.

Later I learned that two of our drivers were relieved from their duty because they were found to be working for the North and the Vietcong. We were lucky they did not take one of the nurses as hostage, especially when coming back to quarters in late evening or early morning from the hospital.

Nurses were also warned not to ride alone in taxis, which were small Renaults. We were reminded that there was a bounty for capture of a Navy nurse. Later, however, I discovered that all nurses did it. It was too inconvenient to wait around for another nurse to share a taxi when you wanted to go somewhere.

My ride arrived and I grabbed my bag. I was curious to see the hospital and begin taking care of patients in Vietnam.

Chapter 13

Naval Station Hospital
Saigon, Vietnam, 1964

I had not seen the Naval Station Hospital before, and it was a shock when we drove up to it on one of Saigon's busiest streets. I thought I was going to a prison. The first building was an old, gray apartment building taken over by the Navy. It had five floors, with very narrow stairways for inpatients and an ICU on the first floor. All the rooms were very small, and the largest held five patients. There was a French-style elevator (open grill) that rarely worked.

Navy Station Hospital, Saigon (BUMED Archives)

83

Directly behind the main hospital building, with outside stairs, was another four-storied structure, with no elevator. This was used for medical and isolation patients. Next was a small office (called the Master at Arms shack) containing phones, dispatches for ambulances, and a place for weapons to be stored when soldiers came in from the field.

A ramp led to a large, one-story building in back that held the ER, triage, and pre-op, and across this room were several tables for operations and a recovery area. Everything was in one large area. There were doctors, a nurse anesthetist, and another nurse, plus several hospital corpsmen; it was very busy. This medical facility provided care for the southern part of South Vietnam. The Army 8th Field Hospital, with one hundred beds, was about two hundred miles further north. (Much later I would be sent there to help.)

Ambulances, jeeps, and trucks with patients were able to drive right to the ER or to a large area for setting up triage outside, if needed. The whole area had a cement wall around it with a high-wire grenade screen; in front of the wall were several Vietnamese women mixing cement. They put the cement in wheelbarrows and brought it to an area where Vietnamese men were waiting. The mixed cement was poured on top of an area, and the men smoothed it out. I would discover that this building of the wall would go on for a year.

For security, there was a guard house just outside the hospital compound. There were also three watch towers, two out back and one on the side of the compound. These were manned with Army personnel 24/7, and often also with Vietnamese military personnel. A large water tower was on the roof. One thing I found interesting: no American flag flying.

Across the street was a five-story building, which was the clinic. The first floor contained the lab, x-ray, pharmacy, and personnel offices. On the second and third floors were doctors' offices and treatment rooms. The fourth and fifth floors contained rooms for some of the hospital corpsmen.

To get from the hospital to the clinic, we had to cross a very busy street, which was also very dangerous. One time as I crossed the street, escorting a patient, a car kept coming towards us. I managed to move the patient, but the car touched my uniform.

A Vietnamese policeman usually stood there in a white uniform (they wore white shorts most of the time), and it was his job to stop traffic so we could cross. Sometimes, if an attempted coup was coming, the policeman on duty would take off his uniform and run away. They were nicknamed "white mice." Later, crossing the street on foot became so dangerous, we had to use a car to cross.

There was no kitchen or dining room in the hospital. All food for the patients was prepared at the enlisted quarters a block and a half away, placed on two carts, and delivered three times a day. The food was delivered to the hospital by two men, who pushed the carts down the street rain or shine. Food was placed on the trays by nurses. This was to ensure that the special diets for patients were delivered. Staff, including nurses, delivered the food. Later, trays were collected, returned, cleaned, and prepped for the next meal.

Staff members were responsible for their own food. The senior nurses would go back to their quarters for lunch if they could, and sometimes the junior nurses returned to the Brink. To make sure the wards had at least one nurse on hand, we took turns staying behind; that nurse usually skipped lunch that day altogether. Some days we could get something off the food cart. Other days there might be a Thai nurse on duty also. Doctors and corpsmen could also leave, but patient care came first, and there was no takeout.

There was a soccer field five minutes away, and it was used as a landing field for helicopters bringing in wounded from the field or transporting hospital patients to the air base for the medical evacuations (medevacs). This started a few weeks after I arrived.

The patients had all types of injuries—from gunshot wounds to burns to injuries from bomb explosions and plane crashes. We also treated malaria and all kinds of disease, including problems found in the States. A common injury involved punji stick wounds. The Vietcong made punji sticks from a piece of bamboo, wood, metal, glass, or anything that could be made into a sharp object. They were covered in feces or other rotten elements and buried in the ground with the point up. After soldiers walked over these and impaled their feet, the wound needed to be cleaned, left open, and watched for gangrene. Injured patients were on bed rest, sometimes for three or four weeks.

* * *

I now had an idea what this hospital was like. It certainly was not new. When it was time to meet the staff, I was brought into a small room with a conference table. The commanding officer, Captain R. Fisichella, Medical Corps (MC) USN, was at the head of the table, and I sat next to him. Other doctors were seated, and the three senior nurses were standing across the room. Once I was introduced, the questions began: who did I know, who did I know in Washington, how did I get these orders (apparently, they were convinced that I had to know someone), and on it went.

Captain Fisichella was very annoyed with me. He had requested a senior nurse with OR experience and what did he get but a Lieutenant junior grade. My blood pressure rose.

"How did you find out about Vietnam?" he asked. "This is an important assignment, and many people wanted it."

I told him I had needed to look up Saigon in the encyclopedia because I had never heard of the place.

"What expertise do you bring?" he asked.

I thought, *"What is wrong with this man? I have only been in the Navy two years."*

I simply said that I had just completed a course on mass casualties with the Army, although I had yet to see one.

I think I surprised him, the expert, with that answer. He looked at me and said, "You are excused." He was stuck with me.

CDR Richman came with me to the Intensive Care Unit and I was assigned to a patient who was a casualty: gunshot wounds, fractures, and tubes everywhere. He was still unconscious. There was no blood bank, so when a patient needed blood, we put out the word through enlisted quarters: blood type X needed, report to the lab (the lab did not have facilities to store blood). If someone had a high fever and needed to be packed in ice, men were sent to local bars to get it because there was no refrigeration at the hospital to keep that much ice on hand. It was challenging.

I stayed away from Captain Fisichella whenever I could that year. I found out he was a transfer from the Army, and the Navy had offered him a promotion. He had just married and did not have time for the honeymoon and had needed to leave his new wife in the States. He was not happy.

I completed the orientation for the hospital and the clinic. One day I was scheduled for the 3:00 P.M. to 11:00 P.M. shift, and when I arrived at the hospital, I heard yelling and saw several of the day staff standing outside a room. An American prisoner had been brought in and was being very disruptive.

He was being held in a padded room close to the ICU and kept banging his head against the wall, saying, "I didn't mean to kill him!" The entire hospital could hear him, and no patients were getting any rest. They wanted to sedate him, but no one would go into the room. He was a large soldier and he could easily harm the staff.

After a while, I said I would do it. The doctor gave me a syringe with a large dose of Thorazine. I took it in with me, hoping I wouldn't stab myself. The cap was on the syringe, which was in my nurse's uniform's pocket. My sweater covered the pocket. I took off my nurse's cap, rank, insignia, and name tag. There was a small window on the door, and I told everyone outside to watch me. I would be on the other side of the room, and if the soldier did go after me, they needed to come in and intervene. I told them I expected that it was going to take me awhile to talk him down.

I went in, and did talk him down. During my talk with the patient, I learned that he had shot a Vietnamese soldier in the back. The Vietnamese soldier had shot the patient's friend, also an American soldier, in the back. The American soldiers had been teaching the Vietnamese soldier, and when the American friend had turned his back, he was shot. Our patient then shot the Vietnamese soldier and was now under arrest for murder.

The patient finally let me give him the injection to help calm him down, and it took a while to take effect. The military police came in and put him in restraints.

I was told that in the morning he would be brought to the airport and sent on his way to the Navy prison in Portsmouth, New Hampshire. Once the security team found out I was from Dover (nearby), they asked if I would go back with them. The prisoner would need to be sedated for the whole trip. They would make sure I got back to Saigon after the trip was over.

My answer was NO. We sent one of the corpsmen to keep him sedated and monitor him. This happened at other times in Vietnam. I always wondered what happened to the American soldier (and others like him) after he reached the states.

* * *

I had been at the Brink several weeks, and a few of the men thought I should try eating out. There was a restaurant across the street nicknamed Cheap Charlie's. I never knew the correct name of the restaurant. The owner had sent two of his sons to school in the United States, and the men said they were going to the restaurant to give the man some business to help support the sons. A group of eight, including one other nurse, went to the restaurant. I did not get a good look at the place and was seated looking out the window. I did not understand the menu, so someone ordered for me. Everyone ordered a drink. No water.

While waiting for the meal, I felt something at my foot and jumped. The man next to me asked, "What happened?"

"I felt something," I said. I had sandals on. He announced to the table that the Vietnamese cat was out, and everyone was to move their feet like they were marching. Everyone started to march sitting down. I thought this was strange but wondered what a Vietnamese cat looked like, as my mother had a Siamese cat.

Later I felt something at my toes, so I looked down quickly to see the cat. What I saw was a large rodent with a long nose, beady eyes, and a long skinny tail. It was a rat at my toes. It moved and I sat back up.

The officer next to me asked, "You saw it?"

All I could do was nod my head.

"Next time, wear shoes to cover your feet," he said.

I thought, *There will be no next time.*

In contrast, The Floating Restaurant (My Canh) was an establishment we enjoyed going to. It was on the Saigon River, and they had a ramp we walked on to get to the restaurant.

My Canh floating restaurant, after the bomb, Saigon

Fishing nets from My Canh on the Saigon River

One day, however, the ramp was blown up. Then we had to take a rowboat to get to the restaurant. It was a good place to sit and watch them bring in the fishing nets.

* * *

Another time, CDR Richman asked me to join her on a trip to Bangkok, Thailand. Most of the nurses had already been there. We left Friday evening by plane and arrived there a few hours later, checking in at a hotel that was used mostly by the military. A large pool was still open, and we swam in it. The next day was full of shopping and sightseeing: river cruise, silk factories, gems, temples, and so forth. On Sunday, we did the same until late afternoon. We were back in Saigon around 8:00 P.M. It was a wonderful break, and I was eager to do it again.

I visited Bangkok three times and went with Eileen the next time. The tour was a little different, but we still enjoyed lots of sightseeing and shopping. Then two of the Thai nurses went back for their two weeks. I had gotten to know them, and they suggested I fly over by myself. They were from different areas, and they would each meet me and take me to see their own part of the country.

I spent all day Saturday with one nurse up north (she had a car). We went to her village and visited the zoo and saw a Bengal tiger that was kept in a cave. The natives ran cans across the bars to get its attention at feeding time. That made me very nervous, as the bars were loose and the tiger shook them; I had visions of that cat getting out. Sunday, I visited the southern part of the country with the other nurse. We spent time on one of the beaches that was a favorite area. (Many years later, that entire area was swept away in a tsunami.) At the end of the weekend, I just made it to the plane going back to Saigon. I felt very lucky to see the country outside of Bangkok.

Temple, Bangkok, Thailand

* * *

Work schedules were like those in the States. Three shifts when possible in the hospital. If I was scheduled to work the day shift and I had the OR call, I worked in the hospital until 3:30 P.M. Then I left the wards and went back to the OR. If a case was going on, I relieved that nurse. When that case finished, I went back to the Brink and waited. Sometimes I was lucky and had no more cases; other times I was there until 8:00 A.M. the next day, when I was finally relieved. Then I helped on the wards for a couple of hours. I had more than a few days with thirty-hour shifts at the hospital.

When working the evening shift, I was the only officer at the hospital unless staff was called in for surgery. As the days passed, I got used to the hospital and had more confidence. When it was quiet, I often went out to the Master at Arms shack (office) to find out what was going on.

The military police often made rounds, so I could hear the news that way. If a battle was going on and casualties were coming, we had advance warning. However, there were times when a truck or jeep arrived unannounced with the injured.

Working in the clinic gave me a little break. I did triage and made sure all went smoothly. Hours were different: 8:00 A.M. to noon, then 2:00 P.M. to 5:00 P.M., with a long lunch. The city closed all the shops at siesta time.

* * *

I had been working in the clinic and doing triage for several weeks with no problems. Some of the senior medical physicians had rotated back to the States, and two young MDs who had just finished their internship reported. Since I was the triage nurse, all patients coming to the clinic had to see me or the Thai nurse and present their problem. I assessed it and wrote an order for lab work or an X-ray based on what I saw or was told by the soldier. This was intended to speed up the process. The patient went to the department, had the test done, and reported back with results. Then he was assigned to see the first available doctor. Patients who needed emergency care were sent to the hospital. Minor treatment was done at the clinic.

One morning the doctor came out of his office and started yelling at me, shouting that I didn't know anything. A room full of soldiers and corpsmen were watching; I was embarrassed. What had I done? He was waving a lab chit. When he calmed down, I learned the story—or part of it. According to the doctor, I was wasting his time (hours of it). Usually, soldiers gave me their symptoms and I sent them on. Unbeknownst to me, however, many of the soldiers were making up these symptoms and then taking the lab tests just to get the chance to see the doctor about their *real* problem: sexually transmitted diseases. Those patients actually needed a different lab request, which the doctor then had to arrange.

I suspected that the men were using this approach as a way to bypass the female nurse so they could speak to a male doctor instead. This caused a lot of extra work for the nurse, lab, and doctor.

I told the doctor I would take care of it and took one of the corpsmen to the lab and X-ray area. I had the corpsman check with a few soldiers who were waiting for testing to confirm my theory and pull them out of line.

My suspicions were right. Most of the patients were eighteen to twenty-four years old, and they didn't want to talk to me. Between all the bars, brothels, and mistresses, they were embarrassed about their real problems, so they were making up all the symptoms they reported to me. To address this, we set up a new line with a corpsman, and I eventually made my way back to the hospital. I still worked in the clinic at times, but that main problem was solved.

* * *

One patient I could not forget. His name, yes, but not his injuries. He was a young Army pilot whose plane was shot down, and he was brought to us with burns over most of his body. He was still conscious but dying. All we could do was try to make him as comfortable as we could.

He was on a Stryker Frame to turn him from back to abdomen to relieve the pressure on his skin. He was given morphine often for pain. We watched as his kidneys shut down, then the rest of his organs. It was very difficult to witness.

I remember another soldier, brought in from the field. There were three injured at the time. Two were already in surgery, and I was helping to get the third ready. As we were taking his uniform off, I found a grenade in the shirt pocket.

All weapons were supposed to be removed before coming into the building. I had the corpsman bring a basin and put a towel in it, and then I gently put the grenade on the towel and asked him to leave the building, walking slowly. Another corpsman made sure a path was clear and told everyone in the room not to move until it was outside. Then, it was removed from the area.

Another day, four soldiers came to the ER with one of their teammates, who was wounded. The senior soldier insisted on being with the wounded soldier and was very vocal about it. We had surgery being performed and did not need a big disturbance about it.

The other men left and went outside to wait. I told the senior soldier he could stand in the corner, but I did not want him to faint. I had the corpsman watch him as I was cleaning the wound. I could see him start to fall. He was caught and then moved outside. The sight of all the blood got to him. Brave in the field!

* * *

I also had patients who made me laugh. They were bored and on bed rest; there was little to occupy their time and minds. Books were seldom around, and the ones in existence, along with a few magazines, had pages torn. The same applied to packs of playing cards: some were always missing. Of course, there was no TV.

One night on the top floor, there was a room with four young patients. I could hear them on the first floor. The corpsman said when I had some time, they were waiting for me.

Unfortunately, since I was the only LTjg and the youngest, I was called "the baby LT." A patient heard it, and I was stuck with the name. They would tell the corpsman they wanted the baby LT.

It was a busy evening, and I did not get to them till later.

One was lying there, hands on chest; the others were on their sides watching. One said he was not feeling well, and I should check his pulse to make sure it was ok. I did and told him he was fine.

"Are you sure?" he said. "Maybe you should check my heart with a stethoscope."

I did and said, "Your heart is beating just fine."

Then he said he thought he had a fever and took my hand and put it on his forehead with a smile. I left it there a minute, watching the others, and then told him that he did feel warm, so I would take his temperature.

The others were concerned that he had caught something and asked if it was contagious. I said I would check theirs also.

I went to get the thermometers. They were glass. But as I was leaving, I said, "It's a shame the corpsman dropped the tray with all the oral thermometers. I have to use the rectal ones."

The soldiers quickly said they felt great and there was no need to check theirs.

"No, I'll check everyone," I said.

I went downstairs, laughing. Nothing had happened to the thermometers. I told the corpsman to check on them later.

* * *

There were times I was asked to go and make an extra check on patients who had been injured. Other times I was asked to check on a young man who was very depressed or worried about going home, fearful that his wife or girlfriend might not want him around anymore. I always made time to sit and talk to those patients. Sadly, some had already received the "Dear John," as we called them.

Watching river activity from the park, Saigon

One morning after a very long and stressful night in the OR, I returned to my quarters at the Brink, but I did not want to go to my room. To get some fresh air, I decided to walk down to the Saigon River. There was a little park and some benches close to the water.

The park was about four blocks from the Brink, and the shops and several bars along the way were closed—or so I thought. I sat on a bench and watched the activity on the river, but gradually I became nervous about being there, so I kept turning around to see if someone was coming up behind me, remembering the bounty placed on nurses.

I decided to leave. While I was walking back, a soldier came out of a bar so fast he almost knocked me down. Instead, he ended up grabbing a light pole, and he kept going around and around it to keep upright. I was not sure if he had been thrown out or was given a running start.

I turned and kept walking, but he noticed me and caught up with me. He wanted to know if my father knew I was out. I said I lived close by, adding that my father did not know, but my UNCLE SAM did.

He continued to follow me, wanting to walk me home. I declined. "Then take me to lunch," he said. Next it was an offer for dinner.

I kept telling him he needed to go back to his barracks and get some sleep. The Brink was almost in sight. I advised him that if he continued to follow me, he was going to be in trouble; the Army guards were just ahead.

The Brink appeared, and I told him I lived in that building.

"That's where all the officers live," he said.

I told him I was an officer, but I don't think he believed me because there were only four females who lived in the building.

I looked young and wore my hair in a ponytail off-duty. I told him again that I was a nurse corps officer, that the guards would not let him go beyond the wall, and that he could be taken away. He waited until I approached the gate, and when I looked, he had turned back. Since he had spent the night drinking, I wondered if he had lost an Army buddy or received a letter that his girlfriend had left him. This was common.

* * *

Another night it was busy at the hospital, and I did not get up to the fourth and fifth floors until late. However, the patients had been quiet most of the evening. When I arrived at the top floor, all four patients were out of bed, looking out the window.

They were supposed to be on bed rest. I coughed, and they each made a dash for their bed. I asked what they were looking at.

Nothing. Was a demonstration forming? No. The youngest was trying not to laugh. I started to walk to the window. They all said there
was nothing out there, but obviously something was.

I went to the window and did not see anything. As I turned,
however, I noticed two men go into the building across the street two
doors down. I turned back to look. A light came on and the shade
was up. Two people in the room with a blue cross on the front door.
It was a brothel. Two doors from the clinic. That was convenient.

I had a mission. I went down to the Master at Arms and asked
the chief for the list of the off-limit establishments. Was this place
on the list? They could not find the list. I did not believe them. Now
they wanted to know my reason for getting the list. Was I looking
for a job? They were giving me a hard time, and then the military
police arrived on their rounds. They were no help. The conversation
ended when a few causalities were brought in. However, a few days
later the blue cross was removed. The city had many such places,
and I remembered my early days in the clinic.

* * *

Saigon was called "Bombsville," because there were so many
bombs. From the time I arrived in Saigon the military presence continued to increase; all I noticed were uniforms and green fatigues.
As the troops increased, so did the fighting, along with our patient
census. We went from one medevac a week at the time I arrived to
three by the time I left.

We had to move the patients to make room for new ones. Sometimes the patients would go to Clark Air Force Base Hospital in the
Philippines. If they were able to go back to the fighting soon, they
would return to Vietnam; otherwise they went back to the States.

* * *

The patients were our priority. We were always busy. There was no extra staff. When we had a day off, we took advantage of it.

One night after eating in the dining room with another nurse, we went out onto the roof patio to get some air. Three younger officers came to the table to talk. Later, the other nurse left. I stayed and we continued talking about the States. They asked me what I missed; I said water skiing. They said they would take me, but I thought they were joking. They weren't. They knew about a place with a boat and skis.

We set a date for the following week. They drove me out in a jeep: it took almost an hour to get to our destination. I was very leery at the end. There was a dirt road and lots of vegetation. Finally, we came to the water and boat. We went down to the dock, and the men kept asking if I could ski. I got up on the skis, and they took the boat down the river. Then I was out in the Saigon River and could see the large ships.

After being out there for a while, I gave the signal to go back the other way. It was quiet. After about forty-five minutes, I noticed that one of the men was sitting at the boat's bow with his rifle. The officer driving the boat was standing and looked very alert, and the third one in back, who had been watching me, also had his rifle and was now watching the river banks. I became nervous and didn't know what they were looking for: the enemy? I was a good target. Or was it the snakes in the water? I gave the signal and was afraid I would fall in the water. I could not get on land fast enough—no more skiing there for me.

I had a few more chances to water ski later, but that was at Nha Trang, on the South China Sea, where some of us would go for a weekend, leaving on a Friday evening or Saturday morning and

Nha Trang, Vietnamese woman on way to market, South China Sea

coming back on Sunday afternoon. We went up on an Army plane, and Eileen was usually with me. These weekends usually involved a day at the beach, including water skiing and a boat ride. It was like being on a lake. In the evening, we were taken out to dinner. A short break!

* * *

Another memory from Saigon that stands out is the street children, who were everywhere. One time I was out shopping, and a group came up to me. The older child put her hand out and said, "You American Lady?"

"Yes," I said.

Darby at orphanage, Saigon

"I touch?" she asked.

I said yes, and she touched my arm. Then she ran off saying, "I touch American Lady!"

About five other small children did the same thing and were very happy. I was not sure what that was about.

Other times, I would see the children and they would say, "Hi, American Lady."

Many nights I returned from the hospital after curfew to find a group of children all curled up in a circle, sleeping in a doorway of some shop. They moved from doorway to doorway. One child, who could have been about five years old, was trying to toilet train a younger child in the street. Many little ones had no diapers.

I did see an orphanage in Saigon, which was run by nuns and had two children to a bed. Those children did have adequate clothing and seemed well fed.

* * *

Shopping on the streets was an experience. I went a couple of times with another roommate and then I was on my own. Schedules prevented another nurse from being available, although safety was a big concern. Most of the items I looked at were on the sidewalk, and then I bartered with the shopkeepers on the price to get them to lower it. It was almost like a game.

When I went shopping, I had to pass the Continental Hotel. It was a busy hotel, where many of the journalists and photographers stayed. Every afternoon they would all be out on the long veranda in rocking chairs having their afternoon drinks and waiting for someone to go by with news. Since they came to the hospital often to interview the patients, they knew the nurses when we walked by, and hoped for news. They often yelled at me to come up and talk with them, but I just kept walking.

The black market was a very large business. When the supply ships came in, the merchandise often disappeared and sometimes could be found on the streets. This included things that were necessary, such as medical supplies, weapons, and uniforms for the men. Cameras and radios were also hot items. One time I was shopping and found several surgical instruments marked US Government or US Navy. I bought a few and thought I would get reimbursed, but no.

In fact, the hospital was short on supplies and certain instruments. One time we were going to do surgery and needed a specific instrument but did not have it. We called the Army 8th Field Hospital, and they sent it down by plane; after the surgery, the instrument was returned.

* * *

Another interesting place was the Central Market, a huge area with a tent-like appearance with little stalls inside. It had everything you could imagine, but it was dark and had many different odors. There were many stalls with men on rugs smoking their long pipes. I only went twice, with another nurse.

Both times there were several men from the BOQ with us. Some waited outside while the others took us through. If we did not return by a certain time, they would go in to find us. It was definitely one place I would not go to alone.

* * *

Soon after I arrived, I joined the Cercle Sportif, a private club. The CDR was instrumental in getting membership for the nurses if they wanted it. The membership fee was small. The building was old French style with lots of shade. It was a place to go for some exercise, with a dining area and game rooms. Two of the activities were swimming and tennis. I took advantage of the pool, and for a while I went in the morning when I was working the afternoon shift. Since it was a place for many Americans, a bomb would go off frequently, and on three occasions one went off while I was there. The first two I barely felt. The third one went off when I was in the pool, and I felt it. That was my last visit to the club.

* * *

In November or early December, I agreed to be a substitute on a date to go to a French restaurant (an expensive one) in place of the lieutenant commander, who could not go. The date was with one of her friends, who had recently been stationed in Vietnam. The restaurant did not open until 8:00 P.M.; there was dinner, live music, and dancing. A table of Army personnel were sitting next to us; our tables were not very close, but they were drinking all evening. We danced for a while, and after we returned to our table, a very tall Vietnamese man who spoke excellent English came to our table and asked my date for permission to ask me to dance.

My date did not know what to say and looked at me. I was not sure what to say, either. Then I agreed, since I was curious: where did he learn to speak such perfect English?

"School in the States," he told me. His family was from Northern South Vietnam. He had been sent to the U.S. years ago for his education. He asked me to go to dinner later, but I declined.

Meanwhile, at the Army table, they were no longer slouched down in their chairs. They did not like what they saw, and once I started back to the table, someone from the Army table started to approach us. If we had stayed, the outcome would not have been very good, but my date got up and we left.

* * *

I had several different and unique experiences in Vietnam. These made my days interesting, and they provided short breaks from my time at the hospital, which was where all the nurses spent many long hours with our patients. The briefer chapters that follow highlight more of these experiences.

Chapter 14

Flying
1964

Since I had flown in Pensacola and enjoyed it, I wanted to see Vietnam from the air. Some of the officers at the Brink said that I could go to Tan Son Nhut Airport on the Army side and ask if they would take me up. I talked Eileen into going with me, and the officers did take us up for a ride. We just needed to be in uniform, so we flew several times, stopping to deliver paperwork or supplies to Army bases that were in the process of being built.

One time, after we had just landed and were making our way down the runway, I looked out the window and noticed a large plane over by the tree line. It was covered in a big black net. I asked the pilot, "What was that?"

He said, "You didn't see anything."

I said, "Of course I did."

He said, "No, you didn't."

I finally caught on. I had seen something I was not meant to see. It was the U-2 spy plane.

*　*　*

Another time while we were flying, shots were fired at the plane. We had to detour and get the plane checked before going back to Saigon. We landed by the coast at a spot where the Air Force was building a large base. Our pilots told us to be quiet; they did not want anyone to know we were in the plane. They received help from the Air Force, and soon a group of men were walking all around the plane, checking for the bullet. It was a very hot day, there was no air circulation inside, and the plane was parked in the sun. We had no water, and inside the plane it was extremely hot. I was beginning to feel the effects of the heat. I asked Eileen to crack open the plane's side panel. No luck. By that point, I was not feeling well at all, so she tried again.

As she continued to struggle to open the panel, it suddenly fell onto a piece of metal we were sitting on—with a very loud bang.

Immediately, five Air Force men peered into the big gap and saw us. One kept saying over and over, "Look, there are women in there. Who are they? Where did they come from?" It was like a broken record.

Our pilots came around to look, but they ignored the questions. They simply said they needed to get back to Saigon and instructed the other men to finish checking the plane.

I asked for some water; with the side of the plane gone and some air circulating, I felt better.

We still had to wait awhile before leaving. Eileen and I decided we were very lucky; If we had landed in the jungle and needed to walk, we could have been in danger because we were not wearing fatigues. We were in our summer uniforms, and we had skirts on. We decided that before any future trips, we would talk with our roommates about acquiring fatigues.

Chapter 15

Designer Fatigues
1964

After discussing our need for fatigues, we had to figure out how to find them, since they were not a Navy nurse corps uniform item. I suggested we tell the senior lieutenant and have her ask the commander if we could find some for all four of us, since we needed them to fly in planes. The senior lieutenant asked, but the answer was no, we should work in our white nurses' uniforms. We went back and explained we wanted to wear them to fly. We were told not to fly, which made us upset. Army nurses had fatigues and worked in them. All four of us complained to Army men at mealtime: no fatigues and no flying.

After a few weeks, there was a knock on our suite door, and two Army men came in carrying a big bolt of fatigue-green material. We would need to arrange for the tailor to make our fatigues, but at least it was a start. We could not be like the Army nurses, so we designed our own. There was enough material for four sets of pants, big shirts, and garrison caps. We also needed patches in black, one for the word *Navy* and the other with our last names to go over the shirt pockets. We were off to the tailor's to be measured. Then we waited.

Eventually our fatigues were ready, but our black patches turned out to be very large white ones.

We did not want them, because everyone would notice these fatigues were not an official uniform. We asked the tailor to repair them, but he refused.

Darby in front of the Brink

We also had to find boots. This quest proved to be impossible, so we tried black loafers. That did not work either. However, our only tie shoes were the white nurses' shoes. At one point we thought we could paint them black, but that did not pan out either. We needed our white nurses' shoes, so that was what we wore on the planes. At last the "white shoe Navy" was back to flying.

(This description is based on old Navy slang: *white shoe* referred to Medical Department–included nurses; *black shoe* referred to those who were seagoing; and *brown shoe* was tied to the aviators.)

If we were flying somewhere and needed to be in the correct uniform at our destination, we just took that uniform with us and changed into it after we got off the plane. No one said a word.

Chapter 16

Navy Nurse Corps Anniversary
Saigon, May 13, 1964

Every year a celebration took place wherever Navy nurses were stationed; it was a Nurse Corps tradition. Our senior nurse decided that nurses in Saigon would celebrate with a tea at the top of the Rex Hotel. We would wear our summer dress white uniforms (like the dress blues).

Invited guests included the Commanding Officer of Headquarters and the Commanding Officer of the Hospital, plus others who had helped at the hospital, our Gray Ladies (officers' wives who worked under the Red Cross), and several more officers' wives who donated many hours of their time to the hospital and the patients. A few others who had contact with the hospital were also invited.

There would be the traditional cutting of the cake with the senior nurse (CDR Ann Richman) and the most junior nurse (me). This was a big affair for the nurses, and I was excited. On the morning of the big event, which I had off from work, one of my roommates said, "You should go to the Vietnamese beauty shop and have your hair done, cut, and colored blonde."

My hair was long at the time, so off I went.

I was there longer than I had planned, and when I returned, my roommates had already left for the tea.

I quickly changed into my uniform and prepared to leave. We had been warned against traveling alone, but I had no other option. Should I walk or take a cab? I decided I would be safer walking,

Navy Nurse Corps Anniversary invitation, cover

The Navy Nurses of Station Hospital
Would be delighted to have you
Join them for a Tea
Given to celebrate
The 56ᵗʰ Anniversary of the
Navy Nurse Corps
Date : Wednesday 13 May 1964
Time: 3 to 5 P.M.
Place: Top of the REX.

Navy Nurse Corps Anniversary invitation, inside

Nurse Corps Anniversary: left to right, LT Carleda Lorberg; LCDR Tweedie Searcy; LCDR Bobbi Hovis; CAPT M. Friedman, CO HQ Support Activity Saigon; CDR Ann Richman, senior nurse; LT Eileen Walsh; LTjg Darby Reynolds; CAPT R. Fisichella, CO Navy Station Hospital Saigon

so I started off. I was about halfway there when a shadow blocked the sun.

A big black cloud. Would it rain? Could I make it to the hotel? If I went back to the Brink, everyone at the ceremony would wonder where I was. I couldn't call. Our phone connection only went to the hospital. I chanced it and kept walking, quickening my pace. The cloud kept getting closer, and then the sky opened and I was soaked to the skin.

Should I go back or carry on to the event? I continued to the Rex and entered their lovely elevator, dripping wet, and left a big puddle in the middle of the floor. When I arrived at the top floor, CDR Richman and others just pointed to the roof patio and told me, "Out. Go out on the roof."

The sun was out, and I went to dry off before the party. My "dry clean only" uniform was drying into odd wrinkles and bunches on its own, and my hair—with all its new beauty salon curls—was now straight and touching my collar (against regulations).

A little later, the party began. I helped cut the cake, and pictures were taken. I couldn't wait to get out of my uniform!

The guests were very amused with my uniform problem. I returned to the Brink and hung the uniform on a hook. It did not look good. I thought, *"I will not be wearing that again."*

Numerous times after that day, my roommates, who had also been at the party, asked me, "What are you doing about that uniform?"

I needed to order another one, but I had no plans to do that. I was not sure if I would leave the Navy at the end of three years. My answer was always, "I'm working on it."

My uniform stayed hidden among my clothes, but people continued to ask me about it. Around September, I got tired of the questions, so I decided to give it to Mama-san to see if she could do something with it. I pretended I was ironing around the sleeves, to remove all the wrinkles. She took it, but two weeks later she came to me crying and very upset. I had no idea what the problem was, so I asked one of the other nurses what had happened.

My roommate brought my uniform in. It was an odd shade of yellow and had shrunk two sizes. It looked like they had wanted to match the cloth and gold braid. It would never be worn again. I tried giving it to Mama-san, but she would not take it. I put it in a trash bag and left the room. After she left, I noticed she had taken it.

Now the nurses were really after me to get a new uniform. It was very expensive to order one. I decided that if I ever needed to appear at an event in the uniform, I would just volunteer to work at the hospital that day instead. I thought that would be the end of my uniform problem, but as I later discovered, that was not to be the case.

I often wondered what happened to my uniform.

Chapter 17

Money Changer
1964

One question that came up soon after I arrived in Vietnam was how to pay for things. I was told that on payday, a Navy officer would come to the hospital and pay the staff in American currency. We would only receive a portion, because they did not want to load Vietnam with a lot of American dollars. These dollars were valuable for the North Vietnamese and especially the Vietcong to be used in trading with other countries for weapons and so forth.

On payday, an Army officer came a few hours after we had received our pay, and another line formed for staff who wanted to convert money to Vietnamese currency. Initially I had no idea how much I needed, so I said $200.

My transfer to Vietnam had cost me money. For instance, I had lost my housing allowance, since my room in Vietnam was provided along with food. Back in the States, sharing with four other nurses, the roommate situation had allowed us to save a little. I was also still making car payments since my car had not been sold. When the Army officer converted my cash, I had to pay him a fee for his service. I thought I was paying him too much, although later I found out we all paid the same fee no matter how much money we changed.

On the next payday, I noticed there were no hospital corps staff changing money, so I asked and found they took care of it themselves, with no middleman. Now I was very upset about the money

I was paying for the service, and I complained to the officers in the dining room about how the senior Army officer was making money on us; I said he should be reported.

The officers said, "Oh no, don't do that." They offered to change mine at no cost.

I didn't like that, so I went back to the corpsmen to find out more about how they did it. They did not want me to get involved either, but they offered again to change my money for me. I wanted to do it myself, but too many shady people were involved.

Another way to get Vietnamese currency was to pay in American dollars then get change in Vietnamese, but I had to learn the going rate and then barter in the exchange. The shopkeepers all wanted the American dollar and would mark things down. It was like a game to barter. At times I could not get the shopkeeper to come down, but then I would leave and maybe try again later. I got quite good at it over time.

Chapter 18

Saigon Coup Attempt
Late August 1964

On days that I worked the 3:00 p.m. to 11:00 p.m. shift, I always had some excitement. One day, it was a coup attempt. The city had plenty of unrest. I was on my way to work and had just entered a Navy car with the Vietnamese driver. A Thai nurse was already in the car. She told me about the big demonstration near where she lived, with mobs yelling at each other and firing rifles. There were also people carrying torches and torching cars.

We had to go around the Central Market, and I saw the same type of loud, very large, and angry crowd. We made it to the hospital and began our shift. It was a very busy evening, and occasionally we could hear gunfire.

Around 11:00 p.m., the night nurse arrived, and the Thai nurse came to me and said she was afraid to go out in the mob. I thought about it and went out to our Master at Arms shack, where the phones were located. I told the chief I was requesting backup to make sure we both got back to our quarters safely. That meant a call to the Army military police.

"Oh, you nurses are always trouble," he said.

I knew he did not want to call the Army. We had a discussion, and I knew how to take care of this easily.

"Fine," I said. "I will find a bed in the OR and the same for the Thai nurse—and since she is a contract nurse, you can explain to the commanding officer in the morning why the Navy has to pay her double time. Maybe he will take it out of your pay."

117

I left then because another patient needed help. The Thai nurse came to check if we were leaving.

I said, "I think so—maybe a few minutes longer."

Soon after that, the military police arrived with soldiers in a jeep. As we were getting into the Navy sedan, another jeep arrived with four more soldiers. The chief went out to talk with them, then sat in the front seat with our driver. We had protection now.

The city was wild, with each side trying to take control. We left the hospital, taking the Thai nurse home first. It was near midnight, and we were close to her area when we ran into a mob. They were burning cars, carrying torches, and shooting into the crowd.

We could not tell who was for the North or for the South. Our sedan was wedged in between the two jeeps, bumper to bumper, and the three vehicles could not move; we were surrounded. I kept looking at the jeeps because I was afraid someone was going to be shot. Would I get out to help or would I be dragged out and taken away? Then a bullet went across our front window. The chief and driver got down on the floor. I was looking around to see if anyone in the jeeps were hit. When I looked back, they were motioning me down.

Then a bullet passed by my door. We sat there for some time until finally the traffic began to move. It was awhile before we got some distance from that crowd. I gave a sigh of relief that no one was injured.

We took the Thai nurse home. Then there was one jeep left to escort me to the Brink BOQ. The other jeep was called off because it was needed elsewhere. I thanked them. They still had a long night. I asked the chief if he had enjoyed the ride. South Vietnam won that one.

* * *

There were several mini coups attempts that year, and the fighting increased with the daily increase of American soldiers. On those days, we always breathed a big sigh of relief just to make it back home.

Chapter 19

United Service Organization (USO) 1964

I made a few visits to the USO in Saigon. I could walk there, so one day I went to see what it was like. It was quiet in the early morning but more active after 10:00 A.M. The men came in for a break. There was air conditioning! We could eat, read, or play games. It was a meeting place.

USO Saigon

I often went to look at the magazines. Sometimes I liked an article or a photo of a piece of clothing, so I asked if I could cut it out. If it was an older magazine, I could do it.

With the photo of the clothing in hand, I visited the tailor to have a dress or skirt made. Otherwise, I shopped at the Exchange at the Air Base, which didn't have much of a choice for clothes. At one point, there was a bomb thrown by the entrance of the USO, and sandbags were placed from the road to the door. It was like going through a tunnel to get inside.

Chapter 20

Sick in Quarters (SIQ)
1964

In the middle of my tour in Vietnam, I developed a staph infection on my face. It started as a very small scratch and continued to enlarge. A hard carbuncle. Staph infections were very common in Vietnam, and I was on two different antibiotics but no improvement. I had so much edema I could not work and be near patients. I was confined to my room at the Brink because there were no rooms for female patients at the hospital. The only person around was Mama-san, who did not speak English.

The doctors did not want to excise it. Instead, they wanted to send me to Clark Air Force Base Hospital in the Philippines, but I really did not want to do that. I suggested trying another antibiotic. Nothing. My face had so much edema I could not see. Commander Richman would sometimes spoon-feed me.

Eventually I had no choice, so I remained in my room at the Brink as I waited for the next medevac to Clark. I was afraid I would not return to Saigon, and I did not want to leave that way.

One of my roommates came to my room at lunchtime. We talked about the hospital, and she mentioned that a new doctor had reported in for a few days to relieve one of our surgeons for some R&R. I asked what his specialty was; she said plastic surgery. He had come from one of the ships. We wondered why a plastic surgeon was on a Navy ship in Vietnam, but strange things did happen. (He was assigned as a general surgeon.)

Then I thought, *"He could remove the carbuncle on my face."*

My roommate helped me get ready, since I could not see, and we went back to the hospital together. She checked with CDR Richman, who asked the doctor if he could do the procedure. He said yes, and since the OR was quiet, he did it right then.

This hard core took up a big space in my cheek. He packed it with gauze and did not suture it, instructing me to let it heal from the inside out and then rub it with cocoa butter. I would not have a big scar and I could go back to work in a few days.

A friend had the same type of infection in Da Nang, Vietnam, but she was far less fortunate. She had a massive infection and spent a long time in the ICU back in the States; she ended up with a large sunken area on her cheek and a large scar. On all accounts, I was lucky.

Chapter 21

Ice Cream
1964

Working with the corpsmen kept us on our toes. They were a young group who were very eager to learn, and I was a big sister to many.

Our days and nights at the hospital were busy, with long hours. We often missed meals, and days off were frequently cancelled, especially for the corpsmen. They never complained, but one day they took matters into their own hands and gave themselves a much-needed break.

When I first arrived in Vietnam, it was the custom for the Air Force flight nurses to bring a tub of ice cream to the Air Base when they came for the medevacs. When the hospital staff returned from the Air Base, they brought back ice cream for patients, which was distributed in the evening before bedtime. This was the only ice cream we received for the patients, so it was a royal treat.

One evening, when it was time for ice cream, a corpsman came to me and said it was missing. This made no sense to me. It had been there in the afternoon. Where did it go? Who had it?

The search was on. Everyplace was examined; everyone on duty was questioned. It was recorded in the hospital log: patients were waiting for the ice cream. All the guards were asked if the ice cream had been taken, but we received no answers. Somebody took it, but who?

Eventually, I gave up. I said, "I will not write anyone up. Just let me know how you did it."

The mystery continued, but three weeks later, I found an anonymous note in my sweater pocket explaining what had happened. Some of the corpsmen had placed the tub of ice cream on the back of a corpsman with a big jacket. He was escorted by another corpsman through security, and they proceeded to BEQ (Bachelor Enlisted Quarters) for an ice cream party.

The guards had not noticed, and I never said a word. They really did deserve a treat.

Chapter 22

The Monkey Episode
1964

One time we were flying and stopped at a base under construction; papers needed to be delivered. The base was practically empty, with only one small building and an outhouse. All the land had been cleared, and the tree line was a distance away. A group of soldiers came to meet us and said others were out on patrol; they didn't know when they would return. We waited for a short time, but when they didn't return, the pilot said, "We need to get back to Saigon."

At this time the men were squatting, smoking cigarettes, and watching us.

I asked, "Can I use the latrine?"

A soldier said, "No; it has just been cleaned and is being guarded."

I asked, "Who's guarding it?"

He said, "A monkey."

I did not believe this and asked to see the latrine. It was located behind the building, so I set off to see it.

Our group—including me, the other nurse, our pilot and co-pilot, plus a group of six men from the base—all walked around the building to see this monkey. He was tied to a long chain that went up to the outhouse, and he was dancing and screeching. At first, I thought I could make it to the door of the latrine safely, but then I realized I couldn't, and I was afraid the monkey would grab my hair or bite.

I had noticed earlier that each time I asked a question, five of the men looked at one man in particular, and I began to think he was the owner of the monkey.

We waited a while longer, and then the pilot said again that we had to leave. I walked over to the line of men and stood in front of the one I thought was the owner.

I said, "You all have had your fun, but if you don't move the monkey in five minutes, then I am going to kill the monkey and you can plan on monkey meat for your dinner tonight."

I looked at my watch, patted my purse, then walked back in front of the monkey to decide on the best shot.

After four minutes, the monkey was moved. I had no weapon, but they didn't know that. We all visited the outhouse, then left.

Chapter 23

Singapore
September–October 1964

Eileen and I took a weekend trip to Singapore. Our schedules were such that we were often free at the same time. This time we flew commercial. We left Friday evening and arrived at our hotel late, but—seeing all the lights—we felt like we were in a big city. We got up early to take a tour; we wanted to see as much as we could. One place we were advised to visit was the Raffles Hotel, the oldest hotel in Asia. Somerset Maugham and Rudyard Kipling had stayed here. We sat in the rocking chairs on the spectacular veranda with ceiling fans; had the famous drink, the Singapore Sling; and watched the other tourists. Then we went to the zoo and other tourist spots, plus we did a little shopping.

One of my purchases was a jewelry box with white jade trim and many drawers of brocade. I was very proud of this because I had bargained over the price. I hand-carried it, but even so I had a very difficult time bringing it back to Saigon. Customs would not let me take it in. One of the Vietnamese agents kept looking at it and smiling, and I thought, *"He wants it for himself."*

We had heard to be careful; things could be taken away. Sometimes you needed to pay extra. I had not seen anything like this jewelry box in Saigon.

On the other side of the building was the American military section. Eileen had already gone through customs. I guess I was loud enough that I eventually warranted help from the military section, because I got through with my jewelry box just as I was beginning to think I was going to have to leave it.

Later, these jewelry boxes were sold in several places in Saigon, but it still remained my favorite token from Singapore.

Chapter 24

Armed Forces Radio Station Vietnam, 1964

One way to receive the news was from Armed Forces Radio; the other was from the newspaper *Stars and Stripes*. I usually had my little Sony transistor radio on most of the time in my room. When we each came back from the hospital, my roommates and I seemed to go to our rooms and stay there; seldom would anyone choose the living room. I was used to listening to the radio and music for company. The news came on every half hour.

Two of the nurses heard that the Exchange had received several Sony tape recorders, large ones with speakers attached. These were not 8-tracks or cassette players, which came later; they had 7-inch reels. A good buy.

The two nurses each bought one, and Eileen and I each decided to get the same ones. We all bought two extra speakers and amplifiers. However, we were not able to buy the music tapes, because when we made it to the base, they had been sold.

I ended up meeting the radio station announcer at the Air Base, and I told him I enjoyed the music. I explained that I had bought a Sony reel-to-reel tape recorder, but I could not buy tapes to listen to any music. He said he could help me: I should buy several blank tapes, then come to the radio station, and he would loan me some of his tapes, which I could then record. I bought the blank tapes and went to the radio station, which was in a trailer.

"Go in back and pick out what you want," he told me. There were hundreds of tapes, all types of music.

I selected some and went back to where he was sitting. He was on the air, so I waited. He noticed I did not have many and asked why I did not have more. I explained that I didn't know what he needed to keep at the station.

He said, "There are duplicates of everything; take more."

I told him I had three other roommates and I needed to make copies for them. It would take some time. We all had the same model Sony recorder. He explained that all four tape recorders could be connected, making it easy to record all of the tapes at the same time. I wasn't sure how to do that, so he came to the Brink and connected all four recorders for us. There were wires all over.

Since the other nurses did not want to put the blank tapes on and remove the completed ones, I acquired a job that lasted several weeks. I routinely went out to the base to buy blank tapes, then selected tapes to record. After I had recorded boxes of music for all nurses, several of the men in the building asked for some. I did a few then quit. In the end, I had many boxes of great music. Some of the songs that were popular in the early 1960s were "New York, New York"; "I Want to Hold Your Hand"; "Hey Jude"; "I Got You Babe"; "Moon River"; "My Girl"; and "The Twist."

* * *

Several years after I retired from the Navy, I had a yard sale. That morning, I put the tape recorder along with the speakers and the amplifier on a table for sale. A woman looked at it and said, "My husband was in Vietnam. He had a tape recorder just like it, but it was lost in his shipment home. He wishes he still had it. He was severely injured and still is in a wheelchair. He does not get out much."

We got talking, and I ended up giving her the tape recorder, the extra speakers, and the amplifier. I then went into the house and brought out several boxes of tapes to be played.

She kept saying, "I can't pay for all this."

I just said, "No, you can't. This is from one Vietnam Veteran to another Vietnam Veteran. I hope he enjoys the music."

She left in tears, saying, "I can't wait till he sees what I have for him."

Best yard sale I ever had!

Chapter 25

The Colonel
Fall 1964

The following episode, which happened sometime in late September or October 1964, was not one of my better moves. It was late evening, and the monsoons had arrived. In fact, it was raining so hard we could hardly hear anything else. I was getting ready for bed and had just taken a shower and washed my hair when I heard Eileen calling my name, so I went out to our living room. She was pointing at a stream of water, which was flowing across the floor.

The water was heading to an alcove at the entrance to our quarters. This alcove held all the purchases that we had made and were storing until we went back to the States: thousands of dollars of merchandise, including china, crystal, stereo equipment, extra speakers, and so forth. If some of the crates got wet and the wood decayed before we had a chance to send them back to the States, all could be destroyed.

Shouting so I could hear her above the pounding of the rain, Eileen yelled that she had called topside twice to the Army for some help. No help. The water kept coming in the apartment. The drainpipe outside our French door had broken, and all the water from the sixth floor was coming onto our balcony and under the door and across the floor. This was a serious problem.

There was still no help for us, so I decided I would try to move the water to the entrance doors and into the hall. Mama-san had a mop.

The elevator, which was right across from our entrance door, had a grillwork door and a shaft; to the immediate left of our door were the stairs to the ground floor. I started moving the water out of our quarters. Eileen was watching me.

A big party was going on topside with lots of drinking. Even with the rain, we could hear them yelling. Curfew was in effect, however, so I knew that no one should be out using the elevator.

Time was of the essence; I really needed to move that water out to the hall. I became so involved with the task, I did not hear the elevator start. There went the water—just as the elevator rose with two people in it. They both got drenched from head to waist. I looked in time to see a full colonel in an Army dress uniform with medals, accompanied by a very beautiful Vietnamese woman in a lovely expensive ao dai, the native Vietnamese dress. They both got a mouthful of water. He did not live in our building.

The elevator stopped at the next floor, and they got out.

I heard him say to the woman, "You wait here, and I will be right back. I have a matter to take care of." Well, I knew what that matter was. I turned to see if Eileen was still there, but she had disappeared. I decided to wait. I was wearing an old chartreuse terry cloth muumuu with all kinds of threads on it. I also had on my shower shoes, and my hair was in big, fat curlers with colored sticks to keep them in place. I was holding my mop and had a bucket nearby.

The colonel called me everything thing he could think of, including words I had never heard.

I said, "You have a disgusting mouth! You need it washed out with soap and water!"

I was thinking, *"And maybe a little lye."*

"You're fired!" he shouted.

"You can't fire me!" I yelled back.

"Who the hell do you think you are?" he demanded. (I think he thought I was the maid.)

"I am Lieutenant junior grade Reynolds, Navy nurse," I replied. "Look at the water and where it is going. There is thousands of dollars' worth of merchandise here. We have asked for help repeatedly, but everyone is too busy getting drunk to help the nurses."

At that moment there was a big roar from the sixth floor—perfect timing.

I continued, "I am going to keep pushing the water out, and probably when enough goes in the elevator shaft it will not work, and perhaps it will go down the stairs. If someone comes down, they might just fall and break a leg or a neck, and guess where they will go? The Navy hospital. And who will take care of them? Navy nurses."

I guess he finally had enough of me. He turned and left. A couple minutes later, the elevator went to the sixth floor. Eileen came back into the hall, laughing.

"Do you think I'll be fired?" I asked.

She was still laughing, then I started, and soon we were both sitting on the couch laughing.

"Oh well, I was thinking of getting out," I said.

I grabbed the mop and went back to work. Eileen came out with her camera. Twenty minutes later, an Army soldier appeared with a ladder, a bucket, and something to reach the downspout. My work was done. I kept waiting to hear something from my commanding officer, but there was nothing. I hoped I never ran into that colonel again.

Chapter 26

Abduction Attempt
November 1964

Four nurses rotated back to the States. First, LCDR (promoted to CDR) Tweedie Searcy, nurse anesthetist, left in late September and was replaced by CDR Priscilla Miller, nurse anesthetist. A week later, LCDR Bobbi Hovis was replaced by LCDR Harriet Langham. Those nurses were assigned rooms with CDR Ann Richman. Next, LT Elaine King and LT Carleda Lorberg were replaced by LT Ruth Ann Mason and LT Frances Crumpton, who were both assigned to the Brink BOQ. That left CDR Ann Richman, Eileen, and me to orient the new nurses. These were difficult and busy times, as there were always bombings in Saigon and troops brought in from the field.

A week or so later, one of the new nurses at the Brink mentioned an item she wished she had brought with her. I thought I might go to the Air Base Exchange, get it for her, and look for some Christmas things.

I decided to shop early on the morning of my day off. Originally, the drop-off and pick-up area for cabs had been located right in front of the Brink's entrance, but for security reasons it had been moved a bit further away. I walked past security and waved my hand toward the line of cabs. The first cab in line didn't move, but the second cab pulled out around it and drove toward me. Without looking at the driver, I opened the door, explained where I was headed, and started to get in. As I sat down, I finally looked up and saw that he had long hair, very strong arms, and a look of so much hatred I could not believe it. I still had my hand on the door handle and the door was not closed. He stepped on the gas, I fell back into the seat, and the door closed.

We sped down the street, and I yelled at him to stop. He ignored me and took streets I was not familiar with.

I thought, *"He's Vietcong. I made a BIG mistake. Where is he taking me?"*

He kept turning to look at me with those hateful eyes, and I kept yelling at him to stop. He was speeding in and out of traffic, sometimes driving on the sidewalk to get around slow traffic.

I thought, *"If he slows down, I will jump out."*

I had no idea where I was. After a while I couldn't look at those eyes any longer, and I decided to move directly behind him. This was to his advantage insofar as he could now see me clearly in the rearview mirror. On the other hand, I could now see out the front windshield, so I had a better idea of what was coming.

He drove all over the place for more than forty-five minutes. Finally, I saw a bridge up ahead, which I recognized. On the other side of the bridge they were loyal to North Vietnam and were known to harbor the Vietcong. The corpsmen had warned me about it. There were some people on the other side of the bridge who were also loyal to the South, but the majority were for the North. I had been told, "If you go over the bridge, you probably will not come back." I thought about the bounty they had on nurses. This driver was going too fast!

I kept trying to figure out how to get out of this. I thought, *"If I pull his hair, he might lose control and we could end up in the water, but he might be a better swimmer than I am."*

Then I thought I could put the strap of my purse around his neck and pull. However, I also realized that with one arm he could pull it back. Every idea I came up with would probably backfire. We were now on the bridge.

Suddenly, I remembered that I owned a weapon, although I wasn't sure if I still had it with me. My uncle had given me a small knife in a leather sheath when I had left for Vietnam. He had told me to put it in my uniform purse and always keep it there. He had been so insistent that I had put it in my purse, and it lay flat on the bottom. I rarely used this purse and had forgotten all about it. To my enormous relief, it was still there.

I placed the knife in my right hand and grabbed the driver by his shirt at the neck. I told him to stop. He just stepped on the gas. We were almost to the middle of the bridge. I couldn't go across; I would be in Vietcong territory. I had the back of his neck in front of me, but I couldn't cut that, so I came down with the knife on his back. However, he didn't stop; he probably only felt a prick. I came down harder the second time. He felt this; I could see his eyes change as I was looking at the mirror. I took the knife and held it out so he could see it—just far enough that he couldn't reach it— and told him again to stop. He slammed on the brakes. I let go of his shirt, opened the cab door, and fell out onto the bridge. I landed on my shoulder and rolled over to my knees.

Once I was out of the cab, he took off with the door still open. I looked behind and saw two cars coming up toward me, so I managed to get closer to the sidewalk and they went right by. I got up and held on to the light pole on the sidewalk. I was shaking so hard. Another car went by, and then I got to the wall on the bridge and looked at the water for a few minutes. I knew I had to move. I didn't know if my cab driver would turn around and come back after he got across the bridge. I needed to get off the bridge.

There were lots of shops, but who were they loyal to? I did not speak Vietnamese, and who could I call? I just kept walking and looking for tall buildings, which I hoped would bring me to an area I knew. I also kept looking behind me to make sure no one was there. In the end, I walked about five miles in the hot sun. I was extremely relieved when I finally saw a building I recognized, and then I still kept walking, knowing the Brink was nearby.

When I reached the Brink, I walked by security to my quarters. It was about 2:00 P.M. Eileen was leaving for work shortly, and Mama-san was busy. I went into my room and took some deep breaths. Then I took a shower and treated my abrasions. I eventually did tell the others, but I did not want to scare the new nurses too much, as they had only been there a few weeks.

We all had been warned about riding in cabs alone. How many times had I done this? How lucky I was.

Chapter 27

United States Marine Corps Anniversary in Saigon November 10, 1964

At the end of October, several of the Marines came to the top of the Brink for dinner, and when they noticed two American females, they asked who we were. When they learned that we were Navy nurses, they came to our table and asked if we had been stationed at Camp Lejeune. The Navy had a hospital there.

I said, "I spent a month there last year."

A few of them sat down to talk. After the other nurse left, I kept talking, and I ended up dating one of them a couple of times. These Marines were waiting for more troops and would be going up North to fight, but before leaving they would have their annual Marine Corps anniversary celebration on November 10. It was being held at the Diem Hong Palace, and U.S. Ambassador Maxwell Taylor would be the guest of honor. I agreed to go; I wanted to see the palace.

A day later, my date told me that the required uniform was summer white. I didn't have one because I hadn't replaced the old one, so I told him I had to work and couldn't go. Such a shame. The next day, all seven Navy nurses received lovely invitations to the event. The three senior nurses decided they were not going, because it did not begin until 9:00 P.M. The commander sent word to the Brink that, since we provided care to the Marines, a nurse needed to go and represent the Nurse Corps.

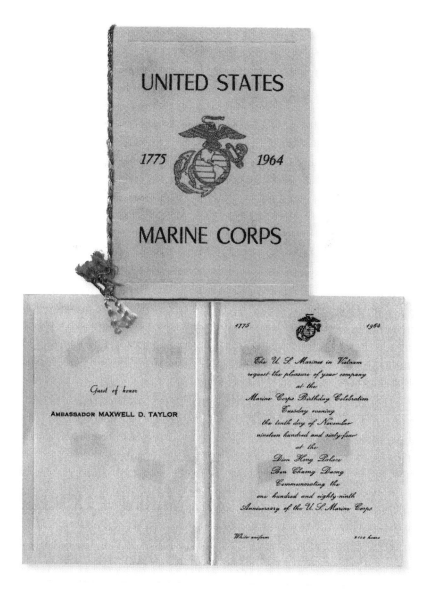

The two new nurses said they would not go; they had practically just arrived. Eileen, who had constantly been reminding me that I needed to replace my uniform, said she was not going either. They all looked at me, and I said, "I can't go; I don't have a uniform."

They outranked me.

When the commander made the request, she did not mention a uniform. I had been selected. Now what? I could not get out of this.

A cocktail dress was one of the items I had been told to take with me to Vietnam. I had brought one, never thinking I would need it, and I had never bought anything to go with it. My three roommates provided all the accessories, from gloves, nylons, and rhinestone tiara to necklace, bracelet, and purse. For shoes, I had to wear my black uniform shoes.

How could I go to the palace by myself? I thought, *"Maybe the Marine who asked me originally doesn't have a date yet."*

I was lucky; he said he could still bring me, and now I would see the palace.

I didn't want anyone to know who I was since I was supposed to be in uniform, so I told my date to introduce me as Miss Reynolds instead of LTjg. Now I just had to get through the receiving line. Maybe no one would know.

It was a huge room full of military, including the Ambassador, a US Marine Corps general, lots of Marines, and the senior officers from other services. A few officers' wives were there but very few other women. The men had been warned not to go to bars and invite the bar girls. It was a long receiving line, and then I saw the Army colonel from the elevator incident. I hoped he would not recognize me.

The room had no air conditioning and was hot. As we came through the receiving line, I noticed a table of officers' wives looking at me. Many of them knew me, so I said to my date, "We should go over there to say hi."

Some were Gray Ladies who donated time to the hospital, and they had also been at the Nurse Corps anniversary when I was caught in the rain. My luck! So, we all had a few laughs.

I was thirsty, so we went to the refreshment table, and I was warned not to drink the punch. I watched them mix a bowl. I could see what was making people so happy. Later, we joined a group of my date's friends, who had been celebrating and enjoying the punch. The group was a little loud. Except for one, they did not know I was military. Then a few senior Marines came over to remind them they were too loud; the ambassador and the general were still at the anniversary celebration, and they had found out who I was.

The conversation changed and we talked about Saigon. The next day many of those Marines would be sent up North to the fighting. The remaining Marines would follow. This celebration would be their last time in civilization for a long time. How many would come back, and how many would be among the wounded?

A couple of months later, Navy Station Hospital Saigon received a request for corpsmen to join the Marines up North. They needed more medical help in the field. These were volunteers; were they ready for the field? Were they prepared to be under hostile fire? Some came to me and asked if I thought they could do it. Hard decision. I was glad I was not making the final call—the one sending them up North to the fighting. They were eager to go and were needed. But would they come back alive?

Chapter 28

Da Lat, Vietnam
December 1964

It was the end of November or first part of December, and CDR Miller had been in Vietnam several weeks and on call 24/7. She wanted a break and had heard about Da Lat, a city north of Saigon in the Central Highlands, but she did not want to go alone. The other nurses were not interested, so I said I would go. I had not been to Da Lat before.

We flew up early Saturday and returned Sunday afternoon. The plane was full of Vietnamese passengers. When we got off the plane in Da Lat, I noticed the difference in temperature and wished I had brought a jacket. I was wearing a sweater. There were a lot of pine trees, and I felt like I was back in New Hampshire.

We took transportation into the city, and since we were so high up, we could see down into the ravines. I could see people down by the stream taking baths and washing clothes. Later we found that they were a native Montagnard tribe who lived off the land and were very helpful to the Americans. After checking into the Da Lat Palace Hotel, we explored the city. We were going to take the bus around the area, but after seeing so many people on it with all their belongings, we thought the bus would land in the ravine.

The fruit market was so large it really impressed me. I bought a large rice basket to carry on my back, and we put all our purchases in it.

Darby at Da Lat Palace

Bus in Da Lat

Fruit market in Da Lat

Meat market in Da Lat

Children in Da Lat

Cyclo in Da Lat

Cyclo in Da Lat

Sunday, we went to mass in the cathedral. It seemed that everyone was seated together on one side of the cathedral, but we chose the empty side. During mass we heard the other parishioners talking; they were all looking at us. Soon after, I heard a noise and looked up; a large chandelier had snapped the chain, and it was coming down. It barely missed us. Everyone turned back, and mass continued. We were nearly killed. I looked around, and several other chandeliers were missing. The cathedral was very old.

After mass, we continued exploring. There was a lot to see.

Then it was time to leave, and more trouble began. When we arrived at the airport, the place was full of Vietnamese passengers going back to Saigon. The pilot and copilot were American. I had never seen so many packages returning. It was not a large plane, and I didn't think all of it was going to fit.

The commander and I stood and watched as they put the luggage in. I was waiting for my basket to go in. The pilot turned to me and said, "You are going to have to leave it, because there is no room."

I was not about to leave it, so I said, "Some of the Vietnamese have several packages; they could leave a few."

He said, "No."

All the passengers were on the plane. They were running late, but I was not leaving without my basket.

I told Priscilla to get on. She really needed to get back because her relief (an MD from the Army 8th Field) had to leave. I explained in front of the copilot and pilot that when Priscilla got back to Saigon, she could tell them the pilot had left me behind, because I was staying with my purchase.

The copilot and the pilot had words. I was very angry, and I told the copilot that I was a Navy nurse and hoped they didn't have a lot

Darby carrying the rice basket

of casualties waiting for me. More words. Finally, the copilot said he would take my basket and put it behind his chair. We finally left.

Back at the Brink, the other nurses really liked my basket because there was none like it in Saigon. Sadly, it was one of my treasures that is no longer with me.

I would later learn that the CIA (Central Intelligence Agency) had American pilots who flew planes in Vietnam and spent time in the area before flying back out. I don't think those two will ever forget me.

Chapter 29

Christmas Eve Bombing
December 1964

December was a busy month. We acquired one more nurse (LT Barbara Wooster) the first week of December, but since our quarters were full, she had a room a few floors above us.

Orders for transfer were always sent out months in advance, and I received orders that I would be returning to the States in March. My time in Vietnam would be over. I had requested three specific places on the East Coast, and then wrote "anywhere on the East Coast" as my next choice. However, my orders were for the Naval Hospital at Camp Pendleton, California.

I went to my Commander and told her she might want to write Washington and let them know I would be leaving the Navy. Because I was a reserve nurse, I could get out when my three years were up—which was also in March, when I completed my tour in Vietnam. I explained that they needed to get someone else for California instead.

She was upset to hear that I might leave the Navy, so she began a chain of messages back and forth to Washington. I told them they would start losing nurses, because two of the nurses who had left previously also had not received preferences they had requested. Vietnam was considered a hardship duty, and after this assignment, we were supposed to be assigned to one of our listed preferences. I wondered, *"Will they change my orders? Do I even want to stay?"*

The holidays were approaching, and the word was out that something big was going to happen All the newspapers, flyers, and Armed Forces Radio sent the same message: "Be observant and check all stray packages." No one knew when or where it might happen. Hospital staff had to be prepared. Everyone was getting anxious the closer it came to Christmas.

A few days before Christmas, some of the men found a Christmas tree for the nurses. It looked rather pathetic since we had no decorations, so we found a few things to add. Then the mail arrived. LT Ruth Ann Mason had been selected for Lieutenant Commander, a promotion. Her letter went on the tree. I also received a letter from Washington. I had been selected for full Lieutenant, and my letter went on the tree.

The five of us decided to have a Christmas Party on the evening of December 23 and invite some of the men. One nurse had to work that night, and it was a small group.

I was scheduled to work the next day, which was Christmas Eve; I was also scheduled for the OR watch from 4:00 P.M. till 8:00 A.M. on Christmas Day. I left the party, and I went to bed at 9:00 P.M. Around 5:00 A.M. I woke up, but I decided I would go back to bed because it was still too early to get ready for work. My door was open a little, and minutes later, someone tried to get into my bed. Since I was wide awake and he was drunk, all I had to do was push him over and he landed on the floor. I told him that if I ever saw him in our quarters again, I was reporting him to the general. What a beginning for Christmas Eve Day!

I dressed in my uniform and went up for breakfast before going to work. From that point on, the day became a nightmare.

I reported to work, and we had a busy day. Around 4:00 P.M. I went out back to the OR to see if there were any new cases. (If so,

I had to remain there.) The corpsmen were cleaning up from the day's surgeries and restocking all the shelves. I thought that since it was Christmas Eve I would stay and help them; then everyone could leave and maybe have dinner.

Tomorrow was Christmas and tensions were high. Would something happen tonight? Tomorrow? There were bets. What time would we be back at the hospital to care for the casualties? Since I had the OR call, they were betting on it. There was a sheet with times, and for twenty-five cents, some of them picked a time. They asked if I would like to put twenty-five cents in the pool. No. They asked one of the doctors who went by. No. Only a few signed up. However, despite the anxiety, everyone was in good spirits.

Shortly after 5:00 P.M., I got a ride back to the Brink. As I was coming into my area, I looked over to my left at a smaller hotel across the way. There was a divider and a street between us. I noticed several women in bright clothes, and they were all laughing. I asked the guard what was going on, and he said they were all part of Bob Hope's USO tour. Then I remembered that Bob Hope had been in a show that afternoon at Bien Hoa Air Base, which was ten miles away, and was also scheduled to appear in a bigger USO Show tomorrow, Christmas Day, at Tan Son Nhut Airport in Saigon. Bob Hope was not with the women at the hotel; I later learned that he had gone off with some members of the military.

I went into my quarters. Ruth Ann and Mama-san were the only two there. Eileen was at work; Fran was out shopping. I rushed in and changed clothes. All the nurses had chipped in for a special Christmas present for Mama-san. We had wrapped it up and wanted to give it to her before she left for home on Christmas Eve. She left our quarters carrying the wrapped gift with a big smile.

About five minutes later she was back, crying, because the guards would not let her go out through security with her big package. They were taking extra precautions to check everyone leaving the building. Either Ruth Ann or I would need to go down and make sure she got out with her present.

I asked Ruth Ann to go, because I was on call for the OR and needed to be near the phone. After they left, I had a bad feeling. I went over to our French door so I could look down at the security line and watch for Mama-san to make sure she left safely.

It was a long wait and I was tired, so I pressed my face and forehead against the cool glass on the door, looking down to the ground floor. Suddenly, an explosion went off! The noise was deafening. The glass of the door shattered on me and the door blew in and threw me into the middle of the room. I don't remember how long I was there; I later discovered I had a concussion.

One side of the French door had blown off and the other side was hanging on its hinges. I just sat there and looked at it. I was covered with glass, but my first thought was that the Brink had been hit. A bomb? I needed to get to the hospital to help. There would be wounded. I stood up and started looking for my nurses' shoes. The big pieces of glass fell off me.

I never thought of myself—just my shoes. I was looking for them; I needed them. I had spent too many nights in the OR in sandals or sneakers on a cement floor only to discover the next day that I could hardly walk.

Two men came in and asked where the others were. I told them that I was alone; Ruth Ann and Fran were outside; Barbara was a few floors above, and Eileen was on duty. They said I needed to leave right away because the building was on fire.

I said, "I can't leave until I have my shoes."

They apparently saw I was not leaving, because I just kept looking for my shoes. I was a little dazed.

They found my shoes and put them on my feet and then each took me by the arm. I think the men also took a few pieces of glass off the top of my head. I found small pieces of glass in my hair for weeks; I would feel something sharp and pull out a small piece. (I couldn't get my hair washed for some time. It wasn't very pleasant.) I also had many small cuts on my fingers

We came out of the front French door into the hall. Both sides of that door were hanging on hinges. The elevator across from the door was not working.

We heard lots of loud voices of people coming closer. We went down the flight of stairs, and as we came around a little bend, I smelled the smoke and then saw the fire.

When I looked straight ahead outside toward the wall, I saw Ruth Ann and Fran. I told the two men I was okay and pointed out the other nurses. The men left and I made it to the wall. I was relieved to discover that Mama-san had gone through security.

The courtyard was filling up with the men coming out of the building, some being carried, others assisted. Some were in their underwear; they had been getting out of their uniforms.

Outside they were put on the ground. More explosions were going off, and the fire was spreading.

I looked for Barbara and noticed her walking out of the building. It was a relief to know that all four nurses were outside. My attention turned to the men on the ground.

I thought to myself, *"Why am I standing by the wall? I need to be over there checking the men. What are their injuries? Do they need surgery?"* I went over to the man on the ground and had to get down on my knees to check him. While I was doing that, a soldier came over, dropped down to my level, and said, "There are many men outside the wall ready to help. What can they do? There are jeeps and trucks lined up also."

I told him, "We need to get these people to the hospital."

The area was almost filled with men sitting or lying on the ground. He said, "I'll take care of it." Another relief!

Our Navy ambulances and the city fire trucks had not arrived. People had been getting out of work for Christmas Eve, and there was traffic congestion. I looked around, The other nurses had joined me and spread out.

The soldier returned and told me the vehicles were leaving for the hospital. All the trucks were filled, but they would be back. I told him I was going with him because I needed to get to the hospital. I got in the jeep and assisted the patients in the back. The other nurses noticed and followed in some of the other vehicles.

Our caravan had not gone far when the ambulances and fire truck passed us. Then, there was a very loud explosion and a huge black cloud. What was that? I learned later several vehicles had exploded. The fire had reached the fuel tanks.

We made it to the hospital in record time. The men driving had the horns on most of the time, and traffic cleared. The hospital heard us coming, and I directed the vehicles right through security to the area in back. Doctors and corpsmen were waiting and helped unload the patients.

The blast had been felt throughout the city; no one had needed to be called. They had all just reported, including the Thai nurses.

Nurses in the hospital were busy moving some of the existing patients to make room for the new ones. Some patients were transferred to Army Headquarters, because they had some beds, and others were moved to the Army 8th Field Hospital.

The other nurses from the Brink went to the main hospital to join the rest of the staff. Patients who did not require surgery were treated at aid stations, which were set up in the hospital or over in the clinic.

I went into the building with ER, Triage, Pre-Op OR, and RR. Our area in back was very busy for the surgeons, the nurse anesthetist, and our hospital corpsmen, and the night began.

After I had been there a short time, a corpsman came to me and said, "I followed you because you are leaving a trail of blood on the floor. You are bleeding from somewhere."

Upon arrival, I had put on a long green gown over my street clothes. (It came down to my ankles.) I was already working on a patient and did not want to stop because I had sterile gloves on, so I stuck my leg out and asked the corpsman if he could see anything on my leg. I could not feel anything.

He moved the gown and told me I had a large laceration close to my knee, which would require sutures. I would have to stop working to get the sutures, but other patients needed attention first, so I told the corpsman to put an ace bandage on it to stop the bleeding, telling him that I would get sutures done later.

As the corpsman was on his knees, putting the ace bandage on, one of the doctors looked over and saw me.

"What are you trying to do, looking up the nurse's gown?" he asked. "We don't have time for this stuff!"

There were more than a few laughs. The corpsman's face turned bright red.

I told the doctor, "I have a laceration that needs to be sutured later, so he's putting an ace bandage on."

The doctor said, "That's okay," and everyone got back to work. It broke up a little of the stress.

We had a couple of interruptions during the night. First, some-one came in and told us that the hospital was the next bombing target, which upped our anxiety. Next, Bob Hope came and visited some of the patients with his sidekick, who fainted and hit his head. (Fortunately, he regained consciousness.)

We worked until after 2:00 A.M., when all our patients had finally been transferred to the wards. Now, it was cleaning time. The whole area needed to be washed and restocked. All the corpsmen went to work. The other staff members went to the inpatient side to check on the status there and then to their quarters

It was my turn to have my leg sutured. I needed help to get up on the table to have that done. Since the wound was right below my knee, the doctor talked about putting a cast on so I couldn't bend my knee and tear the stiches. I talked him out of that and ended up with a thick white wrap from my thigh to my ankle for ten days. I was also checked for my concussion.

When I was about through, they brought another patient in and put him next to me.

I asked, "Why are we getting another patient so late?"

The corpsman said, "They just found two people in the Brink. The floor in their quarters collapsed, and they fell to the ground floor. They were buried under walls and furniture. One was found deceased at the scene, but this patient was still alive."

They had been searching for unaccounted people, but they did not find these men until the fire was out.

As I looked at the man on the table, I asked the corpsman for the man's name. The patient was black from the fire. When I heard his name, I got off my table, went to him, took his hand, and said, "I'm Darby."

The doctor just shook his head, indicating that the patient was not going to live.

Then the man said, "Darby, don't let me die."

He died right after that. His room at the Brink was next to mine. I had eaten breakfast with him many times because we were frequently on the same schedule. He had been like a big brother to me; if I had questions, I could ask him. That was Christmas morning.

* * *

How did this happen? On Christmas Eve 1964, two Vietnamese men in ARVN uniforms drove into the Brink BOQ area and asked to park their vehicle under the building with the other vehicles. They said they were going down the street to do an errand and would return. In the vehicle were 200 pounds of explosives set on a timer. The bombing injured many, including sixty-eight Americans; two people died, and four Navy nurses were among the wounded.

* * *

Around 3:00 A.M., I walked out to the main part of the hospital. I wanted to see what was happening there. Things were settling down. All the new patients were in bed, some sleeping.

Commander Ann Richman, our senior nurse, asked the four nurses if we would like to return to the States. I said no, and the others followed. It was decided that the four of us, who had lost our rooms at the Brink, would temporarily use an apartment occupied by two doctors, who would remain at the hospital. Our more permanent homes would be decided later. We all took a set of OR scrubs so we could change clothes. I kept trying to take the glass out of my hair, because it was getting in my scalp. The Navy car took us to the doctors' apartment. We were tired but unable to sleep.

I was running on adrenaline and thought we should go back

to the Brink to see if there was anything left in our quarters. I was curious since the room next to mine was gone. Initially the others had no interest, but I did finally talk Fran into coming. We went downstairs and woke the driver, who was there with a hospital car in case we needed to go back to the hospital to help there or to receive further treatment for ourselves. He was not happy to leave since there was a curfew. When we were closer to our section of the city, there was a blackout. The bombing had shut the electric grid down.

Security stopped us, but the Brink had lights all around it. The Army had brought out generators and troops to guard the place. In OR greens, with no identification, Fran and I walked as far as we could but were stopped. I told them who we were and explained that we wanted to go to our rooms. Of course, the answer was no.

Then one of the more senior military guards, whom I knew, came by, so I told him we wanted to get to our rooms, take a pillowcase, and fill it up with belongings. We only needed to go one flight up; we could see part of our quarters. I knew I could do it, even with my bandaged leg. He assigned a guard to each of us.

We went into the building and up the stairs. The smell of smoke and the quiet gave me a chill. I went one way to two rooms and Fran did the others. I checked the first room and filled the pillowcase with some essentials—clothes, money, and IDs—and then started to my room. It was at the end of the hall, and I could hear Christmas music.

It gave me an eerie feeling. I asked the guard if he heard the music, and he said that he did. My room was a disaster, with the door half off and everything all over the place. I could not get in. The music was coming from in there. How? Then I remembered that I had put my little radio on when I came back from work. Armed Forces Radio Station was playing Christmas carols. My radio was buried somewhere in the room. The guard and I just stood there. The announcer came on and wished everyone in Vietnam a Merry Christmas.

Then the news came on: the Christmas Eve Bombing, how it happened. He announced the number injured, including four American nurses, and reported that two men were killed (in the room next to where we were standing).

The radio station then returned to the Christmas program. "SILENT NIGHT" was the first carol. It was a SILENT NIGHT. That did it; I had to leave quickly. All that destruction and the two deaths.

My Army escort was with me. I met Fran and went back to our driver and returned to the doctors' apartment. We had a few hours' rest.

Every single Christmas when I hear "SILENT NIGHT," my memories go to that Christmas bombing in 1964.

Chapter 30

Christmas Day and After
1964

Around 10 A.M. Christmas morning, a Navy officer with a truck and a few Vietnamese men were sent to help us move some of our belongings. We had twenty minutes; the building was being boarded up. They were moving us to another building to live in until the Brink was repaired. We took trunks and everything we could carry. Big items we had to leave. I found my fatigues, all my uniforms, some jewelry, my radio (which was still playing Christmas music), and my camera.

I started taking pictures. I wanted to see the room next to mine. I couldn't see it from the hallway door as it was boarded up. With a Vietnamese helper, I made my way over the jumbled mess from my room to the walkway. There was a huge hole in the walkway, so I stepped up on some of the broken cement by the railing and took photos of the room minus the floor.

Three men below stood looking at it. Most of the debris, walls, and furniture had already been removed. They were startled when I knocked a big piece of cement down. (My photo of that was used in several magazines later.) Then our time was up; we had to leave. I was able to take a few more photos as we were leaving.

Darby's room after the bomb

Walkway outside Darby's room after the bomb

Room next to Darby's: two fatal injuries

Side of Brink after bomb

Darby, Fran, Ruth Ann outside the Brink

Ruth Ann and Fran, Christmas Morning, moving day

There were five nurses in our new home: Eileen, Ruth Ann, Barbara, Fran, and me. It was a place I hated and yet don't remember much about. It was in a building that had not been completed. How many floors? Don't know. Occupied already with Army men. The four other nurses were in a different area, and I never saw them in the building. I remember stairs that were more difficult with my leg.

The walls were damp, the sheets were damp, and I had a very light blanket. The electricity was spotty. If the electricity was on, the air conditioning made the room very cold. If it was not on, the room was in darkness. There were no windows, and it quickly got very hot. The temperatures went from one extreme to the other. I needed a flashlight, but there were no extra batteries. There were no locks on the door. I used to barricade my door at night. The bathroom was down a long, narrow corridor. I never saw any security.

I don't remember where we ate our meals; the hospital didn't have a dining room. After moving in, I was on bedrest (because of my concussion and leg injury) in a very small room full of boxes and other items. I didn't know anyone in the building, and the nurses were all working except for Fran, who went to Clark Air Force Base Hospital for surgery on her ears because of the explosion. Mama-san apparently was sent to work in our new building also, but I never saw her the five weeks we were there

One night, I had had enough. The next morning, I got dressed and found my way to the hospital, where I said, "I need a job. I will sleep in that building at night, but I will not stay there during the day." I found a spot where I could sit, keep my leg elevated, and help with OR trays and sharpen some of the needles. Anything to get out of that building.

* * *

Soon after Christmas, some engineers from headquarters came to the hospital and said they were going to check out a Vietnamese hospital that was not being utilized and see if the Navy could use it. They asked if anyone from the hospital wanted to go with the team to look at it. All hospital personnel were extremely busy. So, since I was not doing patient care, I was able to go.

Two cars made the trip. It was about an hour's drive, and when we arrived at the hospital it looked like it was in the jungle, on a long dirt road with greenery all over. The windows were open with no frames or screens; it was in malaria country.

The team left to do their inspection and I started to look at it from the nursing side. I came across one room with an unused medicine cabinet stamped "U.S. Government." Then, I walked into a very large room that could hold fifty patients. It had one patient. Two Vietnamese women were with him, and they looked like they were cooking, either breakfast or lunch. I walked down and the women smiled at me. The patient was a double amputee. He looked happy to see me. I went closer to see his stumps as there was no dressing. I saw something moving and then took a closer look: maggots.

This was nature's way of debridement. I could see where the dead skin had been eaten. I just smiled at them and started to move around the room. I noticed a trench around the perimeter, about a foot and a half deep and wide. I could not get to the window as I had to jump over it. I didn't know the reason it was there. By this time the team had caught up with me, so I asked them. It was the sanitation (human waste) system. A hose was connected to a faucet and the trench was flushed with water; the waste went into the field behind the hospital.

I left them and came to some doors at the end of the large room. The team was with me again and they said, "That is the OR, but you don't need to see it." Of course, I did.

Then we heard the helicopter; it sounded and felt like it was on top of us. I opened the OR doors. In the middle of a very large room was one table with four people standing around it with a patient on it. One light was suspended from the ceiling. The helicopter sounds diminished, and then the four people left the table and went to the end of the room and opened the door, revealing the helicopter. They went out to the helicopter and brought a patient back to the OR, put the patient on the floor, and resumed the surgery with the patient on the table. The helicopter started up with its deafening sounds and left.

There was no way the Navy hospital would be moved here, and no one was interested in lunch. I told them to just take me back to the hospital.

Chapter 31

Purple Heart Award
January 1965

For another week I was still slightly immobile because my leg was still wrapped, but I found a way to get around and was able to help on the first floor in the ICU. Then I managed to climb a few stairs and, when the elevator was working, get to a few higher floors. The physician stated I was "returned to duty in view of need of nursing help in care of other casualties."

One of the Army patients from the Brink asked me when the nurses were going to receive their Purple Hearts. As far as I knew, we were not going to get them. We were nurses doing our jobs. That was what we were there for. The next day, another patient asked the same thing, and a third Army patient had the same question.

I told him I knew nothing about it. I got curious and asked CDR Richman; she also knew nothing about it.

"The Army thinks we deserve it," I said. "Maybe because we are women."

She said she would check.

A couple of days went by. Then we were notified that the next day, January 8, we would each receive a Purple Heart. They said we needed to be at Navy Headquarters for Colors at 8:00 A.M. and we needed to wear our summer blue uniform. I asked if we could receive the Purple Heart in our white nurses' uniform, since nursing was what we were there for. The answer was no.

Because I had decided to get out of the Navy, I wanted to remember this time in Vietnam. The next day was scheduled to be my day off. I thought, "*Will I go?*" I didn't need a ceremony. Fran Crumpton was going to receive her Purple Heart in the Philippines, where she had been sent for ear surgery, so she was not going to be present at the ceremony.

About 10:00 P.M. that evening, I heard a knock on my door. It was one of the other nurses, who said, "We are supposed to wear our white nurses' uniforms." I was happy they had changed their minds, but I wondered, "*Why?*" I didn't have a clean uniform and couldn't wash my hair. I was not pleased with that but I had no choice.

In the early morning, the hospital car took all three nurses to Navy Headquarters for the Purple Heart presentations: Ruth Ann, Barbara, and me. I thought that because I was the LTjg, I would be the last in line, but instead I was the first to receive the Purple Heart from Captain Archie Kuntz, USN Commanding Officer, Headquarters, Naval Support Activity, Vietnam.

I really did not hear what was said as my thoughts were in a different place that day. After the nurses received our medals, some of the other Navy personnel who were present received their own Purple Hearts, and then the ceremony was over.

Photographers were there and we were interviewed. The photographer from the Associated Press asked if I would like a copy of the picture of the three nurses, and I said, "Yes, I would like a copy."

LTjg Ann Darby Reynolds congratulated by Capt. Archie Kuntze, CO of Navy Headquarters Support Activity, Vietnam following award of a Purple Heart

Purple Heart Medal

The announcer from Armed Forces Radio offered me an audio copy of the ceremony. I was happy to receive it, since I had not been able to focus well on the presentation. That is one thing I still have: the Purple Heart tape in its box from Saigon. I have had copies made from that. Here are the words from the ceremony:

Purple Heart Award

Presenter: Captain Archie Kuntze, USN. Commanding Officer U.S. Navy Headquarters Support Activity Saigon, Vietnam

Presentation of Purple Heart Awards to First Women Members of the United States Armed Forces to Receive Combat Decoration for Injury or Wounds Received in Vietnam.

Presentation took place January 8, 1965

Purple Hearts were awarded to LT. Barbara Wooster, LT. Ruth Mason, LTJG. Ann Reynolds.

"Good morning. Before making the awards this morning I would like to say a few words about the medal you are about to receive. In a sense it is the most meaningful and the oldest award for personal sacrifice in service to our nation. It was first authorized by George Washington during the Revolutionary War to recognize the suffering at Valley Forge. It is presented to service men and women who have suffered physical injury or death as a result of hostile action.

The Purple Heart is given by the President on behalf of the people of the United States in gratitude for your sacrifice in defense of freedom.

I should also like to note this is a singular event in Vietnam. Among you are three of the four nurses who were wounded in the Brink explosion. The fourth Lt Frances Crumpton who is in Clark Air Force Base Hospital for treatment of her wounds. These four will be recorded by historians as the first women members of the United States Armed Forces to receive the Purple Heart in Vietnam.

I should also like to make special note of the fact that although wounded in the Brink explosion these women disregarded their own wounds to care for the other casualties both at the scene and later at the station hospital. Their actions in this regard were beyond the call of duty and in keeping with the highest tradition of the United States Navy and the medical profession.

My congratulations to all of you on behalf of the people of a grateful nation."

Associated Press

The first American women decorated for service in Vietnam. (from left) Lts. Barbara Wooster, Ruth Mason and LTjg Ann Darby Reynolds receive Purple Hearts for their wounds in the December 1964 Hotel Brink bombing.

Chapter 32

Army 8th Field Hospital, Nha Trang February 1965

It seemed we were busier every day while Fran remained in the Philippines. I was getting anxious to move back to the Brink. I hated the room I was in and spent more time at the hospital. The first part of February, we moved back to the Brink and our old rooms. The room next to mine was still empty. That memory will not go away.

After we had been back at the Brink a few days, Fran returned. She now had hearing aids.

At that point, I was only weeks away from completing my year in Vietnam. One day, after I had just arrived back in my quarters after a long day at the hospital, a call came. Fran and I were to pack a bag. We were being sent to the Army 8th Field Hospital (two hundred miles north of Saigon) to help. The car was on its way, and we would meet two hospital corpsmen at the airport. Last instructions: "Wear your fatigues." We were glad we had had these designed, although we had never found boots to fit and still had to wear our white nurses' shoes.

We both went to our rooms and started packing. Barbara came into my room to say good-bye. She said, "I will be gone by the time you return."

I didn't understand what she meant, but she didn't explain. (She had just reported to the hospital in December.)

Fran and I made a dash to the car, which rushed us to the airport. The corpsmen and the plane were waiting, but at the last minute there was a delay while needed medical supplies were gathered. Once they arrived from the warehouse, they were packed in the small plane with the six of us: the four medical personnel, the pilot, and the copilot.

When we were flying up, it was dark. We could see flares from a distance, but initially I thought it was thunder and lighting. The closer we came, I realized it was intense shelling, and we were headed right to it. Then the radio crackled with instructions for us to land on a short runway without runway lights. There were airfield people on the ground to guide us in. It was a blackout. No vehicles were allowed on the scene.

After we landed, a guide was sent to escort us to the hospital, and we had to walk with our bags. With the big guns we could feel the ground shake. We were told the VC (Vietcong) were trying to take control of the runway. The escort was yelling, "Nurses and medics coming in!"

On both sides of the runway were trenches filled with our troops. There was also small arms fire.

I came too close to the trench, and a hand went out and grabbed me by the ankle to make sure I didn't fall in. Someone yelled, and the escort grabbed my shirt. When the next flare went up, I noticed I had almost gone head-first into the trench. That scared me.

I didn't have time to think too much about it, though, as all five of us had to keep moving. Then we went into a building, all in darkness. At the hospital, we were in a very large ward. The escort had a flashlight, and it was full of patients. The flares continued to go up. I tried to look around.

Then the escort asked us both, "Would you like a .45?"

I asked why he was offering us guns.

He said, "The Army nurses were issued one; the Army expected to be overrun."

It was understood that the nurses would have a choice: shoot themselves, shoot the enemy, or be taken captive. However, Fran and I both declined the offer of guns. In this dark room I was afraid I might shoot the wrong person or shoot myself in the foot.

The escort needed to get back to the plane to help unload the supplies. He went as far as the door but then turned around, came back a few steps, and said, "If you change your mind, at the nurses' station there's a line of rifles ready to go."

I asked him, "Where is the nursing station?"

He told me, and as my eyes adjusted to the dark room, I could see the rifles. He left. Not a good feeling. Could I use one?

The four of us from Saigon stood there talking. We all wondered, *"What is next?"*

Then at the end of the ward we saw two lights, which started moving our way. It was two Army medics.

I asked them, "Where are the nurses?"

They said, "Out back," which meant Triage, Pre-op, OR, and Recovery. It was just the two medics in the room. I sent one back to tell them that two Navy nurses and two corpsmen had just arrived and needed to know what they wanted us to do. He came back with a list.

First, all patients needed antibiotics. I decided to break us up into teams, but I soon found that the medics were so new they didn't know how to mix the meds. It was time for a mini class. I taught one medic and Fran taught the other, then our corpsmen watched them a few times. Soon the medics were ready to be on their own. Six were giving injections. Catch up time. Every six hours for antibiotics, pain meds, dressings, and IVs—whatever was needed.

All night the shelling, flares, and small arms fire continued, sometimes right outside the door. Each time a soldier opened the door to come in, we would freeze. Sometimes they would yell, "Is everyone okay in here?"

Sometimes we did not know if the soldier was one of ours, or the enemy. I wondered, *"Will we be shot or taken as captives, and will all the patients in the beds be killed?"* It was a stressful night for all, especially the patients, who could not get out of bed.

Sometimes an Army nurse would check on us. Around 5:00 A.M., the nurses began to finish out back and return to the ward. We told them to go get some rest since we were in our routine and things were stable. Later, we were relieved for our break. The corpsmen were given a place to sleep, and Fran and I had a room. Our fatigues were taken and washed. We decided not to wear our white nurses' uniform; the fatigues were more practical.

Around 4:00 P.M. we were back on duty. All the nurses were back, and a schedule was established. The good news was that the Army was pushing the enemy back into the hills. The fighting continued, but the shelling was not as loud.

There were times when patients would wake up, look at me, and ask, "Where am I?" "Am I in heaven?" or "Who are you?" They did not recognize our fatigues.

I answered, "I am a Navy Nurse helping out, and you are in the Army 8th Field."

Most of the patients came from a base in the Central Highlands called Pleiku. They had been attacked the day before—with over 125 injured and 8 killed—and the wounded had been brought down to the 8th Field Hospital. Meanwhile, fighting was going on outside the hospital, as the enemy was trying to capture the air strip at Nha Trang.

I had one patient I will always remember, a young Army captain who was a pilot who had been teaching a Vietnamese student to fly. He had been shot in the back, and he knew he was dying. I tried to spend as much time with him as I could, and I kept him as comfortable as possible. At one point he requested to speak with someone in

Darby with Hospital Corpsmen Paul Farmer, HN USN
and David Scharff, HN USN

Intelligence. I put the request in for him but told him I was not sure
he would see anyone because of the fighting. Since his condition was
deteriorating, he decided to tell me instead. When I was off duty he
died, and later the intelligence officer arrived. I was called in to relate
his story. Then I had to fill out papers and was told not to repeat
it. I was very angry with that. After the war I did mention it, and
there were many stories that were the same: teacher shot in back by
student. This also reminded me of the prisoner I had medicated and
who was sent back to the States when I had first arrived.

Darby and Fran waiting for transport
from the Army 8th Field back to Saigon

The four Navy personnel stayed until the 8th Field staff were back to a more normal routine. The Navy hospital had requested we return to Saigon. The fighting had shifted to the South. More wounded and we were needed back at our own hospital in Saigon.

I had my camera with me, and while we were waiting for our transportation back South, I took some pictures of our little group. (Some were used in military magazines later.) We were happy to return to Saigon.

Chapter 33

Hong Kong
February 1965

During my time at Nha Trang as I had worked with all the casualities, I had also changed my mind about leaving the Navy. I was a good nurse, I had lots of experience, and the war was escalating. My orders were changed and I received a new assignment to the Naval Hospital in Portsmouth, New Hampshire. Well, that seemed a little too close to home for me, but it would make my mother happy.

Eileen was also scheduled to return to the States soon, so we planned to take our R&R trip to visit Hong Kong together while we still had the chance. However, the hospital was so busy, we had to put the trip on the shelf. It was disappointing, but we understood. Then the hospital said that we could go but not together. Only one night would overlap on our leaves.

Eileen said, "I'm still going to Hong Kong." She was more senior, and she was used to travel. I decided to make the trip also, since the military had a hotel with many rooms and lots of tours. I thought that when I arrived (which would be on the night before she left), I'd meet her for dinner, find out what activities she had enjoyed, and then do the same. At night I would stay at the hotel and catch up on my sleep.

When the time came, I went to the airport, a room with many soldiers waiting. Again, I was the only female. At least I was in my summer uniform this time. They were all on one side watching me.

Then a few senior ones came over and asked if I was waiting for someone. They seemed surprised that my answer was no.

Several of the men were looking at my one ribbon on my uniform, the Purple Heart, and one asked, "Were you one of the nurses in the bombing?"

Then the discussion began: Why was I was there by myself? I explained, and I also told them about the 8th Field. Finally our plane was ready.

Eileen was not there when I arrived at the hotel in Hong Kong, but she had left a message for me to meet her at 9:00 p.m. in the dining room. Between her last-minute shopping and packing, we had about an hour for her to fill me in. She wouldn't have time in the morning because her flight was due to leave very early; she was scheduled to work the p.m. shift.

While we were in the dining room, a few of the Army officers came to our table and told Eileen that they would keep an eye on me and make sure I got back to Vietnam safe. I went to my room while she continued her packing.

The next morning, I went down to sign up for tours. Hong Kong was a wonderful place, and I was able to enjoy my time there thanks to all the Army personnel. My entire trip I had escorts, and I was included in their tours day and night. In fact, I was able to see many interesting things and places I would never have managed without these escorts. They also walked me to my room at night and checked it before I went in.

I sometimes went out with one group in the morning and a different group in the evening. In some of the clothing areas, they asked me to try on items they wanted to purchase for their wives, mothers, sisters, and girlfriends. I watched to see what particular requests some of them had been asked to purchase, and so I did my shopping also.

In fact, I did so much shopping, I was running out of money, as were several of the men. Some decided on the last day to take an afternoon ferry tour that went from Hong Kong along the coast of China, and I agreed to join them. We learned that the ferry stopped at the island of Macao (Peoples Republic of China). However, we were instructed that no military were to leave the ferry, although a small boat was available to take other passengers over to Macao for four hours to shop or gamble, which the island was known for. That boat would bring them back to our ferry for the last trip of the day back to Hong Kong.

It was a nice day, and when we stopped to let the other passengers off at Macao, three or four young Army soldiers made a dash to the small boat and set off for the shopping and gambling. The senior officer was furious. They had no passport or visas. What if they found trouble? And would they return in time? The ferry left, and we continued our tour, which was quite enjoyable.

When our ferry returned to Macao, the small boat returned with the other passengers but no Army. Once again, the senior officer was furious. We needed to sail back to Hong Kong. Time was up. There was a schedule, and the military were leaving for Saigon very early the next morning. The senior officer started pacing the deck. He had to pay extra for the ferry to delay its return.

By that point, all of us were anxious and watching for the troops. Other passengers needed to return to Hong Kong as well. Two hours later, a small boat brought them back. I went to the other side of the ferry when the senior officer was talking to them. They were in trouble—and they hadn't even won any money!

At the end of the R&R, I returned to Saigon with many wonderful memories, and I was grateful for the help of the Army men who had made it possible.

Chapter 34

Leaving Vietnam
1965

When my plane from Hong Kong arrived in Saigon and headed down the runway, I noticed the medevac plane. I wondered, *"How many are going out? How busy were they while I was away?"*

When I went into the terminal, I asked one of the men, "How many?"

He told me, then added, "We have an important one."

I said, "Who is that?"

He said, "The chief nurse from the hospital."

That threw me. I was shocked. I asked if he knew what had happened, and he said, "I heard maybe a heart attack."

She was already on the plane, which was preparing to leave. I was not able to see her. Commander Richman had been the one who was at the airport to meet me when I arrived in Saigon and had to put up with me. Several times during the year I had been invited over to the senior nurses' quarters for dinner. I had always enjoyed those times as I learned a lot about Navy nursing with CDR Richman; Tweedie Searcy, the nurse anesthetist; and Bobbi Hovis, who had been a Navy flight nurse in Korea.

She had reported a week before me, and we had both been planning to return to the States together. We had planned to fly to Germany, go to the coast, and take the ship across the Atlantic to New York. She was from New Jersey, and I was going to New Hampshire for duty.

185

I went back to my quarters, thinking I would find one of the other nurses. I did, but Eileen's travel orders had arrived and she had also returned to the States. Another shock. Her relief would be there the next day.

A new senior nurse had also been ordered in. She would arrive in a few days. Since all the nurses had come after me, I was the senior nurse timewise. It was my turn to leave now.

I had identified a few items I wanted to buy and bring back to the States with me, but I never had the chance. The new senior nurse reported in. The next morning, I was told I would be leaving the following morning. Things were changing, and I had the night to pack and ready my room. My replacement would arrive the next day, and I would fly out on the Rear Admiral's plane to Naval Air Station Sangley Point in the Philippines. I would spend the night there, and then in the morning I would be brought to Subic Bay and stay in the nurses' quarters at the Naval Hospital.

Four days later I would board the military transport ship, the *USNS (United States Naval Ship) General Edwin Patrick*. This was a MSTS (Military Sea Transportation Service) ship. The ship was leaving Japan and would stop at Subic Bay on its way back to San Francisco.

I thought, *"I am leaving!"* My friends had all left. I was ready.

Two of the doctors wanted to take me out to dinner, followed by a farewell party at their apartment with some of the hospital staff. We had been through some difficult times. These doctors had just finished their internships before coming to Saigon. In part of my own shipment of belongings from Saigon to the States, I had agreed to include a few items for one of the doctor's parents, who lived in Massachusetts. He was seriously involved with a Vietnamese girl, whom he would later marry. Eventually I brought the items from New Hampshire to his parents.

That night we went to a Japanese restaurant that had Kobe beef. I decided that since it was my last night in Saigon, I would dress up. I wore my ao dai, the Vietnamese native dress I had fallen in love with. I also had gotten some made to take back to the States. It had a snug high-collar top and flowing fabric panels in front and back with long sleeves. Under that I wore silk trousers. This was my first time to wear it, along with my Vietnamese hat.

After a wonderful meal, we went to their apartment, where several staff members had gathered. Long into the night, we were still talking about our days together. Then I realized that we had lost time and it was after curfew. Anyone out during curfew would be shot.

I needed to get back to finish packing and clean my room. The new nurse would occupy it that day. I needed to get this done. A Navy car would pick me up at 6:00 A.M. to take me to the airport. The admiral's plane was leaving at 7:00 A.M. I could not be late!

But how would I get across the city? The only way was on a motorcycle. Going fast, could we miss getting shot? Maybe. One of the doctors had a motorcycle, and so off we went. I had never been on one before.

I kept thinking, *"This may be my last night."* As we went through the city, I heard someone shout, "Stop: I'll shoot!"

I heard shots fired. The city was quiet except for the motorcycle and gunfire.

We were approaching the Brink, and the guards were out with their rifles; ever since the bombing, they had been on high alert with the gunfire. We went flying right through the opening. The doctor who was driving had a tropical shirt and looked like an American, but I was dressed like a Vietnamese (although I had lost my hat).

I yelled to the guards, "Don't shoot! It's Lieutenant Reynolds!"

They came over and said, "Is it really you, Lieutenant?"

I confirmed my identity and then told them I was leaving in a few hours, going back home. I said, "You can relax. I'll be out of the country."

They thought I was kidding. They had come to my rescue a few times.

Then one said, "We'll give you an escort to the Air Base."

I said, "No, I'm going in the Navy car."

I went up to my quarters to get ready. I only had a short time. The doctor came with me and went to sleep on one of the two large couches in the living room, which we had used in the past for Army nurses who visited on weekends.

At 6:00 A.M. everyone was still sleeping. I put my suitcase outside the door, and the driver took it. I waved good-bye to the guards. I was on my way!

Chapter 35

Journey Back to the States
March 1965

Imade it to the airport at Tan Son Nhut a few minutes before the admiral arrived. It was a small plane but very nice. There were only four people: the admiral, his aide, the pilot, and myself. The aide sat as copilot during takeoffs and landings. I had a seat with a window.

After takeoff the admiral asked me, "Would you like to fly over Saigon before leaving the area?" I said, "No, thank you," and I explained that I had been flying several times with the Army. So, we started for the Philippines. It was a beautiful morning, and soon we were over the South China Sea.

Once at cruising altitude, the admiral asked, "Would you mind changing seats with my aide so I can talk with him?"

I gladly agreed. Since I had been stationed at Pensacola, Florida, where all Navy pilots have some training, and then in Vietnam, I thought sitting in the copilot's seat would be interesting.

Later, the pilot asked, "Would you like to fly the plane?"

I said yes, and I had the controls for a few minutes.

The plane went down several hundred feet, and the admiral yelled up front, "What happened?" The pilot responded, "The nurse is flying the plane."

The admiral said, "Maybe you should take the controls now."

That was the end of my flying. I was thankful; I thought I was going into the ocean.

When we got closer to the Philippines, I returned to my seat in the back, and the admiral asked me, "Would you like to fly over Bataan and Corregidor, to see where the Army and Navy nurses were held as captives during World War II?"

I knew the history of these nurses—some had been held thirteen months or longer—and I wanted to see the area. We landed at Sangly Point, Philippines. I felt like I was really on my way home. I spent the rest of the day there.

The next morning, I was taken across the island to Subic Bay, where the ships came in, so I could wait for my ship, the *USNS General Patrick,* a military transport.

I was scheduled to stay at the Nurses' Quarters for four days. As I was checking in, I ran into a couple of nurses who had just come off duty.

They asked, "Are you the nurse from Vietnam?"

They had been expecting me, and they all wanted to know what it was like in Vietnam. After I unpacked a few things, I went with them and met several other nurses. I was included in the group for the next few days.

The nurses told me how to sign up with Special Services to see the island, and they identified the best places to visit. My days were full of sightseeing. At night I was with the group at the Officers' Club. One night we took a trip to see the city called Olongapo, the notorious red-light district outside the gate. My time went by quickly.

When my ship arrived from Japan, I brought my things onboard and found my cabin, which still left me some time to meet my new friends back on land before the ship was scheduled to sail. I learned that I would be sharing a cabin with a mother and two young daughters, who were three and five. They were en route to Hawaii to meet the father, who was taking his R&R time.

USNS General Edwin D. Patrick (TAP-124)

The mother asked if I would mind taking a top bunk, because she wanted to keep the younger one on the bottom. That was fine with me, and I did have a porthole.

Since I had most of that evening free, I went back to say good-bye to the nurses at the Officers' Club. The ship's nurse, LCDR Ruth Halverson, also came over to the O Club for dinner. We met, and she said she would be with the ship until we docked in San Francisco.

We left in the late evening and sailed all night, coming to the island of Guam in the morning. The LCDR found me that after-noon and said, "I'm going to the Officers' Club on Guam to have dinner with the Navy nurses there, and you are invited." Again, everyone wanted to know about Vietnam.

After Guam, there was a long stretch before we reached Hawaii. I tried to keep out of the cabin, so the family had more room. It was very small. They had a bout of seasickness and the mother was kept busy. There was also another family on board with two young daughters. Both families knew each other, and the children played together. They were all en route to meet the men in Hawaii.

For several days I walked the decks, used a folding chair to sit out there, and watched the sea. I was usually close to the lifeboats.

One day as I was sitting on deck, there was a very loud noise, and I was so startled, I fell off the chair, which immediately collapsed. As I found myself sitting on the deck in uniform, a sailor went by and asked what had happened. I told him I'd heard a loud noise.

He said, "That's the ship's horn. The ship was sending a signal to the other ship."

I had to ask, "What ship?" I could not see anything.

He pointed toward a dot on the horizon. He said they would send a signal and our ship would return one.

I am sure he had a few laughs. I was still very nervous with loud sounds.

Sometimes the LCDR would arrange to meet up with me, and we would talk about the Navy and shipboard nursing. I had lost so much weight at the end in Vietnam, the ship's staff kept trying to put some weight on me. With ice cream, they succeeded.

When we reached Hawaii, the families left the ship to meet the fathers. Now I had the entire cabin. The ship was almost empty.

I was tired of this slow boat and wanted off the ship, but there was still another five days to go before we'd reach California. I asked if I could fly from Hawaii back to Boston. I was told that I had orders and could not do that. I offered to pay my own way. The answer was firm: I was going by ship! Because of customs, we couldn't even get off the ship to walk around. After being on this ship I decided to cross ships off my list of possible assignments in the future.

My time on the *USNS General Patrick* gave me lots of time to think back on my days in Vietnam. I later learned that one year after I left Station Hospital Saigon, which opened in October 1963, it turned its keys over to the Army in March 1966, and all patients were sent to the Army 3rd Field Hospital Saigon Vietnam, which was previously the American school. Some of the remaining Navy staff were either assigned to Naval Hospital Da Nang, Vietnam, or to one of the hospital ships—*AH Sanctuary* or *AH Repose*—off the Coast of Vietnam to complete their assignments.

As I considered my time in Vietnam, there were some good memories. However, there were also those I wanted to forget, though I never could. One big question remained: why was I even sent to Vietnam?

I also had many memories of days when I felt more like an Army nurse than a Navy nurse. This had started with my time at Brook Army Medical Center in Texas and continued with my flight over with the Army troops, my residency in the mostly-Army Brink BOQ, and my hospital patients, who were almost exclusively Army. In fact, Saigon was mostly filled with Army uniforms. My duty at the Army 8th Field hospital and my R&R trips had also been weighted with people in the Army. It was time for me to get back to the Navy.

To distract me from these thoughts, LCDR Halverson had a suggestion for me. The Army troops were coming on board—several hundred. They were going to California to bases, where they would have some training and then go to Vietnam. The ship's mission would change. It would stop carrying civilian passengers and convert to all military. She believed I would find it interesting to watch them board. With nothing else to do, I went outside and found a place right above the gangway. Then I saw them, all lined up further down the pier in formation. They marched down to the ship and, one at a time, went up the gangway and then below deck. Hundreds, all in uniforms.

As they were marching, one soldier was frequently out of step. I was primarily watching the pier but would come back to this soldier. After a while, I lost him, but later I happened to look down and he was coming up the gangway right below me.

I looked at his face and was shocked. Here was my very first casualty in Saigon. He had left on the Medevac plane and the staff had wondered if he would make it and if he would lose his leg. I could only see part of his nametag. Did I really have the right patient? The LCDR came to join me, and I told her his story. She offered to check for me since I could not go below deck.

A few days later, LCDR Ruth Halverson caught up with me. She had been very busy, as there was a medical holding company: a company of soldiers who had medical problems and were not ready for full duty. They were going to Letterman Army Hospital in San Francisco for medical treatment, and they also needed treatments below deck.

She confirmed that the soldier I had seen was my patient. I wanted to meet him again. She planned for him to be brought above, and the ship provided punch and cookies while I caught up on his past year of many surgeries. Just seeing one of my patients up walking after we had thought he would lose his leg suddenly made the long trip worth it. Later, when I was settled, I wrote to some of the other nurses to let them know of his status. They in turn contacted him.

Finally we were told we would be approaching the California Coast in the early hours, with docking in San Francisco to occur around 8:00 A.M. I was so excited, I said to myself, "*I am going to be the first to see land.*" I was in my dress blue uniform. It was the middle of March and cold. I went out on deck and found my spot. It was dark.

Around 3:00 A.M., I could hear voices. I was not alone. In a very short time, the place was crowded. A lot of people had had the same idea. Someone spotted a light, and the cheers went up. Everyone wanted to see the light in the distance, so the side of the ship was packed. In fact, there were so many on one side I was afraid the ship would tip, but I was told not to worry. Eventually it was daybreak. Then we were going under the Golden Gate Bridge, but it was so foggy, no one could see it. We were headed for the pier. At 8:00 A.M. we were docking.

I went to my cabin for a last check. My suitcase was already in line to be brought ashore. Then I left the ship, went through customs, and headed for Personnel with my orders to get a ticket to Boston. Almost there. Once I knew when I would arrive in Boston, I called my mother to let her know. She, along with my aunt and uncle, planned to meet me at the airport and drive me back to Dover. After I spoke with her, I finally headed for the airport. I felt a little strange walking through the airport in uniform. Several people looked at me and made some comments, but I was in a hurry and just kept walking. I was eager to get home.

Chapter 36

Back Home: Naval Hospital Portsmouth, New Hampshire March 1965

When I came back home to Dover, I had two weeks' leave and then needed to report to my new assignment: Naval Hospital Portsmouth, New Hampshire, at the Shipyard. My mother wanted me to live at home, and I wasn't sure that I could get her to change her mind. Portsmouth is only ten miles from Dover, and half the city works in Portsmouth. Her reason? I would save all this money.

Actually, it was a good idea since I did not save while in Vietnam, buying out the Orient. I would have to think about that. In the meantime, I needed to buy a car so I could drive to work and start looking at the newspaper to see what was available for rentals in Portsmouth.

I bought a Chevy and, after looking at rentals, decided I would keep my mother happy. I would be at the hospital working, and with travel I would not be in the house that long. I also had not put my Lieutenant bars on yet, as I had not been in long enough and needed a billet (opening in LT rank). Then my salary would increase. My mother was happy, but I was not too sure that her Siamese cat felt the same way.

I reported to the hospital and met the staff. Again, I was the most junior nurse and the only LTjg. A couple more months and I would drop the junior grade. Even though this was close to Dover, I had never been on base. The hospital was medium size and there were no wounded from Vietnam. There was a brick building for those on active duty or retired and a white wooden building down the hill for their dependents.

I was assigned to the brick building for orientation, and later I worked with the dependents. It was very quiet compared to what I was used to.

After a few weeks, my sister, who was now working in the City Clerk's Office, told me that I was going to receive the key from the City of Dover and a proclamation from the State House in Concord. This was going to take place after the City Council meeting, which was soon.

I had been told to expect some publicity, so I agreed. The next day she told me that the city manager's daughter was also going to receive a key. I asked her what the daughter had done: she had been accepted as a Playboy bunny for the new Playboy Club in Boston, which was considered to be an honor for the city.

I told my sister that if they thought I was going to appear in my dress blue uniform with my Purple Heart standing next to the bunny with her big ears and pompom, they were out of their minds. I warned her that if they even tried it, I was going to write an article for *Foster's Daily Democrat* and the *Union Leader* and return the key. That was an insult to the men who were dying in Vietnam.

This dialogue dragged on for another couple of days, at which point I said, "I will not attend." The city manager's daughter could have the stage. I felt better. Unfortunately, it was not over. The next day, a couple of the council members who were veterans of WWII and Korea were in the City Clerk's office and heard the story. They told my sister that they would make sure I was there. When I heard that, I wondered, *"How?"*

The next morning at work, I was called to see my chief nurse, a commander. She told me that she and the commanding officer, Captain

Tuttle, had been invited to attend this ceremony in Dover, which included three guest tickets for dinner and drinks at one of the restaurants. Well, there was no getting out of this now. The evening arrived and the Navy in uniforms were enjoying a meal and drinks. I should actually say *two of them were.* I was a nervous wreck. We were late.

Finally, we arrived at the chambers. My mother thought I had been in an accident. The city manager and daughter were not there. The acting mayor presented the key. My aunt had prepared a reception to follow at her house. The Navy decided that since it was late and a working day in the morning, they would head back to Portsmouth. It was over.

Moving forward, I became the designated driver for my chief nurse, who did not own or drive a car. Whenever a function came up and she needed a driver, she called me. I would finish my shift, go to Dover, change, and drive back to the Nurses' Quarters for her, then take her to whatever place she needed to be. I was always included in her military activities, so I met several senior officers from the main base and those visiting from Washington.

What a change from Vietnam! I needed something to do. What if the corpsmen received orders to Vietnam? They were not ready. They needed more training. I started teaching some of the corpsmen on the ward at report time, and that kept me occupied. I rotated to all the nursing wards, military, dependents, and the Operating Room during my time at Portsmouth.

The hospital also had a prison ward for military patients who were inmates of the main Portsmouth Naval Prison, which was known as the "Castle." There were bars on the windows and the door going into the ward. It was an open ward and you could see the patients/prisoners without going inside. Marine guards were there 24/7 to let you in and out of the ward as needed. It was an interesting ward to work on. Many of the prisoners would talk about their lives and what brought them to the Castle.

* * *

Eventually, two younger nurses around my age reported from the hospital ships, which meant that I was no longer the junior nurse. One day I was called into the chief nurse's office. I had been there a little over a year. I thought, *"Now what?"* There is always a reason.

Commander Harrington told me that the Head of Navy Nurse Recruiting in Washington was looking at me for recruiting duty because I had been to Vietnam. I told her I wanted no part of it. I reminded her that I was a reserve nurse USNR (United States Navy Reserve), and I said that I would leave the Navy if they gave me orders as a recruiter somewhere.

This was a difficult time for me, and whenever I watched the news about the fighting in Vietnam, I would end up leaving the room. I did not want any reminders of Vietnam, yet I also wanted to be there helping because I knew there was a shortage of nurses. In my anger I took all my many boxes of slides I had photographed over the year and destroyed them. (Today I am upset with myself for doing this, because I have only a few that escaped my wrath.)

My commander said she would tell Washington I was not interested in the position.

My recruiter had brought me on active duty as a reserve nurse USNR as there were no United States Navy (USN) Nurse Corps billets open at that time. Now the Nurse Corps was looking at involuntary release from active duty for several nurses who had not been promoted a number of times and who were not keeping up with changes in nursing. These nurses were blocking new nurses from being brought on active duty, as there were no USN billets available. There was a selection board for release of these nurses.

They were also looking at the reserve nurses (USNR) on active duty. If USNR nurses wanted to remain on active duty, they had a better chance of doing so if they became United States Navy (USN) instead of USNR. Nurses also had to apply for this; there was a selection board for these nurses, which was called an augmentation board, and the deadline was fast approaching.

The head of the hospital personnel office, who had been in Vietnam, wanted me to apply for USN status. I resisted, because as a reserve nurse I could be released easier, and I was not sure I wanted to remain in the Navy as a career.

One of the new nurses from the ship said, "You shouldn't bother; you will not be selected anyway."

I knew she was applying, and she did not want me to apply. I continued to think it over.

On deadline day I walked to the hospital personnel office and asked, "What would I need to do to apply?"

He asked, "Are you sure?" He reminded me that this was a commitment.

After I confirmed my decision, he walked to his desk, opened a drawer, and brought an envelope to me. He opened it and said, "Sign where I marked the X's." It was my record and request.

"You had this ready?" I asked.

He replied, "I was hoping you would change your mind." He said that he would get the time stamped and promised it would go out before midnight.

Then I waited. Several weeks later, the list came out. The other nurse and I had both been selected.

It took some time for the paperwork to arrive, and it required more signatures. Finally it was official; I was USN.

A short time went by, and again a call from Navy Nurse Recruiting in Washington came to the front office. They were looking at me for recruiting duty again. Because of my new status, I could not say no this time. I was told to expect a call that afternoon from a nurse recruiter, who would interview me for the position.

This was 1967, and there were more casualties. I thought, *"Where will I end up? Maybe I won't be selected."*

The call came. The Navy nurse recruiter was from the Boston office. She asked me to meet her halfway for dinner so she could interview me. Then her report would be sent to Washington. Recruiting was moving fast.

The next night, I met with LT Anne Barker Nurse Corps USN at a restaurant. We were both lieutenants, but she was senior to me. The interview took place over dinner, and all went well.

At the end of the evening, I asked her, "What's next?"

She said, "As far as I'm concerned, you have the position, but it is up to Navy nurse recruiting and where you will be assigned. They will be in touch."

All night I thought, *"Where will I end up?"*

In the morning, I told my chief nurse about the interview. That afternoon, she received the call from Navy Nurse Recruiting and then told me. I had orders coming for Navy Recruiting Station Boston, where I would be working with LT Anne Barker. I would remain in New England.

I had about six weeks before reporting. During that time, I needed to finish things at Portsmouth, find a place to live, buy some furniture, and move. I looked at one place in Boston and brought my aunt down to see it.

She asked a passing policeman, "If you had a daughter, would you want her living there?"

"NO!" he said.

We found another place. I ended up in Malden, Massachusetts, and I was in New England for the next three years.

Chapter 37

Navy Nurse Recruiting, Boston, Massachusetts 1967–1970

I was settled in my apartment in Malden. It was a new building, with three floors. I had a basement apartment. There was a small swimming pool, but I didn't think I would have time to use it because of my schedule. I drove to the MTA (Massachusetts Transportation Authority) station, left my car, and took the MTA into Boston's Government Center. Then I walked a short distance to the JFK Building, which had twenty-four floors, and took the elevator to the twenty-third floor. The top floor was for Senator Kennedy, and the FBI was below.

It was time to report and hand over my orders and records. I met both my new commanding officer, Commander Bill Elder, USN, and the executive officer. There were three other officers and the nurses. The rest of the office consisted of several enlisted personnel and office staff. It was a friendly group.

I shared an office with LT Anne Barker, Nurse Corps, USN. In a way I had two senior officers: I was attached to the Navy line (instead of staff) and CDR Elder, who was in charge of Navy recruiting for all of New England. He had quotas to meet, and he wrote my evaluations. In Washington, a Nurse Corps, Captain was in charge of Navy Nurse Recruiting. Either way, recruiting nurses for the Navy Nurse Corps was a number one priority, as it was for the Army and the Air Force. Vietnam and the wounded made it so.

LT. Darby Reynolds

There were thousands of casualties. Nurses were needed overseas and in stateside hospitals. The draft brought the men into the military, though some did volunteer.

The job was stressful, because quotas were important for the Navy, which included evaluations and promotions. We were in competition with other recruiting stations around the country every month. It was nothing like nursing.

My orientation took several weeks. I started to be Anne's shadow. It was all new. The office was responsible for five New England states. The nursing school visits included the Army and the Air Force Nurse Recruiters. A program was presented, and each branch told about their corps and what made them different. One program all branches had in common was the candidate program where the student nurse in a college, if selected, could have her junior and senior year's tuition paid for along with a stipend. Hospital school nurses had their senior year paid for. After graduating and becoming an RN, they owed time to the military. It was a good program, and in the days to come I spent a lot of time talking with the students.

When I first arrived at recruiting, the office had scheduled me to be a guest on two television stations. It was for their morning talk shows. I asked the CO what I was supposed to talk about or not talk about.

He said, "Talk about Vietnam nursing, and answer any questions they ask."

The television stations were happy with the interview, and I was very candid. They both wanted me back, but when I returned to the office, I received another reaction: too candid. I had a radio talk show to do, but the senior officers weren't too sure what I would say about Vietnam. It was cancelled. That was a relief.

My first solo school visit was close by at one of the largest nursing schools: Massachusetts General Hospital. Anne had been scheduled to do it but for some reason was not available. First, I had to sign out the Navy car and prepare all my school packets (information on the Navy Nurse Corps). The other military branches did the same. Then I went down to the basement for the car. I knew it would come to a head. All the Navy cars were standard shifts, with the exception of the CO, XO, and the Head of Enlisted Recruiting.

I was NOT going to drive a standard shift. My days in Florida had taken care of that. I took the keys and all my forty-plus information packets and went down to the garage. The CO and XO cars were there, but I could not take those, and the other car was missing. I went back up and told my commanding officer I could not go since no automatic shift was available and I only drove an automatic.

He said, "Then I guess you can't go."

I reminded him that the Army and Air Force would contact all those student nurses, who would not be seeing the Navy Nurse.

He was furious. He called the XO in. They didn't know what to do. They were not giving up their cars. I had a suggestion. The office had a young sailor helping out as he completed his final period of active duty before being discharged from the Navy. I suggested the sailor drive me over to the hospital, which was not far. They agreed. The sailor presented an impressive appearance in his white uniform. I gave him my packets to carry, and off we went to the hospital.

We were lucky to find a parking spot, and I had him come in with me. He carried all my folders down to the front of the class and I took them. I told him he might as well wait for me; otherwise he would just need to return to the office and then come back for me. I asked him to have a seat in the back of the classroom.

The other two recruiters wanted to know who he was, and I said, "He is my driver." During our presentation, several of the student nurses kept turning to the back of the room for another look.

After class, the other two nurse recruiters said they were going to talk to their COs and see if they could get a driver. I knew this was a one-time event. At least my CO knew I would not drive a standard shift, but he was not too happy with me. However, my car problem was solved. I always had a car with an automatic shift when I left the office.

* * *

After a few more months, I finished my orientation with several days on the road with Anne. We made a stop at the Recruiting Station in South Boston to check on applications. It was around 5:00 P.M. on a Friday, and we were both anxious to go home. As we went into the office, someone told us that Washington was looking for Anne, the senior one. Since I was an Ann also, but went by Darby, they sometimes got us mixed up. Washington wanted her to call back immediately. I thought, *"This cannot be good."*

I assumed something had happened to her family. She went into the office and made the call. I was waiting outside when she came out. She definitely had some bad news. She was white.

I asked, "What happened?"

She said, "I have orders."

I thought, *"She is leaving; this will affect me also."*

I asked, "Where are you going?"

She said, "Da Nang."

Although I had lived in Vietnam, I had not been up north to Da Nang; that hospital had not been open when I was there. Even so, I knew this meant Vietnam and Tet, which was not the best place to be going to.

She added, "I have to be in Newport, at the Officers' Club, Tuesday noon. There will be other nurses from New England, and that is the meeting place. A bus will take us to Quonset Naval Air Station, Rhode Island, and then fly us to DC. More nurses from the South will join us, and then we head to California to pick up more nurses and on to Vietnam. I have to see a lawyer on Monday about a will and a POA (power of attorney), then get all my immunizations. I have the weekend to pack."

She did have a roommate, so she would not have to leave the apartment for someone else to close.

I said, "I'll help. We will do it, and I will take you to Newport on Tuesday."

Then I asked her if they had mentioned a relief for her.

She said, "No relief is coming."

I had the five states. I just knew it. I would be alone. There was a shortage of nurses in Vietnam, so now the push for nurses was really on.

That night I went over to her place, after stopping by my own, and along with her roommate, who was also a nurse, we set to work helping Anne prepare to leave Tuesday morning.

I drove her to Newport, where she joined several other nurses in Navy uniforms who were ready to leave. No one had families close by, so I was the one sending them off from Newport. It was another sad day. Everyone had tears in their eyes. As I watched the bus leave, I wanted to be going with them, but I knew that would never happen. I already had done my time.

* * *

A lot of traveling was involved in recruiting, as many hospitals had their own three-year nursing programs for the diploma nurse, and the colleges and universities had the four-year BSN degree. Each time I did my big trip, I left Boston and headed for my first stop in Portland, Maine. Then I went to Augusta and Bangor, moving on to northern New Hampshire, followed by Burlington and Montpelier in Vermont, then down to Western Massachusetts, on to Providence and Newport in Rhode Island, and finally back to Massachusetts.

Places that were a two-hour drive would be a day trip. A nice benefit from the longer trips was that I usually stopped for an overnight visit with some of my former classmates: Brenda Meehan and her family in Western Massachusetts, and Judy Lynch and her family in Vermont. It gave us a chance to catch up on our busy lives.

My long hours and my bad back problem became an issue that landed me flat on my back at the Chelsea Naval Hospital in Massachusetts for one month. During that time, I was in neck and lower back traction and could not get out of bed. I received visits from my office every day to sign paperwork. Being in traction was no fun; there was not even a TV. However, the ICU was two doors down the hall, so I did get lots of visits from the staff.

Some of the doctors wanted to talk about Vietnam; others just wanted to sit in my big easy chair and rest for a short time. Whenever the staff had a party, all the leftover food was brought to my room and put on several over-the-bed tables. Then the night crew would come in for the food. I was always awake at night. At the end of the month, I was on the road again. There were demonstrations against the war that had started on some campuses and I would be stopped before going in and told by security they could not guarantee my safety in the Navy car. This always made me angry, but I would return later.

Some of my talks with the nursing students took place in the evening, after they finished their study hour, which could be around 7:00 P.M. to 8:00 P.M. That meant I would not get back to Boston until 9:30 or 10:00, at which point I would still need to return the car and the keys to the lock box in the office and then take the subway to my car in Malden. I was getting tired of this routine, especially since the men in the office left early.

One evening I returned late and drove to the basement garage but could not find a Navy parking spot, which meant I was going to have to park out on the street and then return the keys to the twenty-third floor before going home. I decided to drive around again and check the cars in all the Navy spots. Since the government cars did not have radios, I had created several mind games to occupy my time while driving. One was to memorize some of the license plates and identify which government office the cars belonged to. While checking the cars, I found one that did not belong in our section.

Okay, I was tired, so I parked right behind the car that did not belong in our section and went straight home. I didn't return the keys, because there was another set that should have been returned by the previous driver of my car. It was very late by the time I got to Malden, and the next morning, I decided to go to work a little later. I had so much comp time I could have had two weeks off, but that is not the way it works.

My secretary called and asked if I was coming in.

I told her, "I will be just a little late."

Five minutes later she called back and said, "You had better come in soon."

I asked, "Is there a problem?"

She said, "The head of the Boston FBI is in the CO's office because you blocked the FBI car. He could not move your car."

I thought, *"Oh! That is a shame!"*

I asked, "Where is the second set of keys?"

"Not there."

I thought, *"Never replaced? Can't find the previous driver? Oh shame!"*

She asked again, "When will you be in?"

I said, "Later than I thought. I need to go to the cleaners with uniforms and have to take the subway."

I thought, *"Here I am again; it used to be trouble that landed me in the chief nurse's office as a young Ensign in Pensacola; now it's trouble with the commanding officer."* Car problems! Another black mark.

Well, after I eventually made it into the office and he expressed his feelings about being talked to by the FBI, I told him it might happen again. I said that if I was returning after dark and it was late, I would do it again; I was not going to park on the street. In fact, maybe I would no longer do night talks with the student nurses.

I proposed that he should allow me to drive the car home and return it in the morning. I pointed out that the Army and Air Force nurse recruiters had cars for late nights. I added that the men in the office left at 4:30 P.M., so maybe I should do that.

I won. I was allowed to take the Navy car home after night talks.

They ordered another car with an automatic shift for the office. I was there for three years.

I did find out what the FBI agent looked like, although we did not officially meet, and one morning when I left the garage, I spotted him driving in front of me. We were both out on the Mass Pike and he stopped at a Howard Johnson's. I decided to pull in also and took a seat at the counter next to him.

When I had my coffee, I turned to him and asked, "How are things with the FBI?"

He turned to me and said, "How do you know I am with the FBI?"

I said, "It's on your car."

He turned around quickly and looked at his car. Paid his bill and left. I had my morning laugh. Thanks to him, I did get the car.

* * *

Once a year around May 13, the anniversary of the Navy Nurse Corps, I visited the governors' offices in each of the five New England states. They each signed a proclamation making May 13 Navy Nurse Corps Day in their state. There was usually a writeup in the newspapers; it was part of the publicity I had to do. There were usually other Navy Nurses with me who could be in the photograph with an article on the Nurse Corps.

I also had to attend special events. One time, the Navy battleship *Fall River* was taken out of mothballs in California and brought to Fall River, Massachusetts, and the city had a big celebration. A ceremony was held on the ship. The Navy personnel were in summer dress whites.

I had to introduce Martha Ray as one of the speakers. She was a comedienne who often toured with Bob Hope, and she had been an Army nurse in World War II. Another time I commissioned a porpoise. Now that one was interesting! I nearly fell in the tank. There are many other photo opportunities I still remember.

One of my favorites happened one summer. I had signed up several Nurse Corps candidates who had graduated and were now RNs and could be commissioned in the Navy, plus a few other RNs. I asked the head of Navy Nurse Recruiting in Washington, Captain Murray, if she would come to Boston to do the commissioning of this group of new Navy nurses on the ship *USS Constitution*, also known as *Old Ironsides,* in Boston Harbor. It took some planning to get everything in place, but all went well, even the weather. Captain Murray and I were in our dress whites. All the new Navy nurses thought the event was great, and so did the parents. They were given a tour of the ship, and it made a good photo op.

* * *

Another assignment that I had was called Casualty Assistance Calls Officer (CACO). This was very difficult, and it was a duty I had never expected to have. The Marine Corps had so many notifications to make—too many killed in action (KIA)—that the Recruiting Station was called upon to help.

All the officers had to take a call. One day I was not in the office, but as soon as I returned, I was given a name. I went out to meet the widow: a young woman with an infant. The initial call with the chaplain and notification had already been made. I arrived about one hour after them at a place in South Boston. When I rang the doorbell, it was answered by a young nineteen-year-old mother holding a crying infant. She could not talk, because she was sobbing. I was in uniform and told her who I was. She could see the Navy car.

I asked if she was alone, and she nodded her head. I then asked to come in, and she opened the door. Once inside, I told her why I was there, and I explained that I was also a nurse. Her family was several states from her, and her husband's family was devastated. We sat on the couch, and I took the infant for a feeding and diaper change.

The mother and baby continued to be my assignment, which included making military funeral arrangements and dealing with all the paperwork after. I was there for her during the wake, the church service, and the burial along with the honor guard. The funeral and "Taps" were very difficult for me. I needed to present the flag. It was early April, and instead of rain there were big wet snowflakes, for which I was thankful. Some of her family did make it to the funeral, and her husband's family was there also. We remained in contact for several months.

* * *

I spent a large amount of time in the office talking to prospective applicants, sometimes by phone or visits when they were in another city. In other states, I also took them on tours of hospitals. I brought one group of nurses to New London, Connecticut, so they could see an active base. This included a tour of the Naval hospital and a submarine, and a visit to the Officers' Club. I was able to get rooms for them at the BOQ, so we stayed overnight. Some of the hospitals' young ensigns were my helpers, and they were available to answer questions for the prospective Navy nurses.

Applicants had to have physicals, and then I had to work with them to prepare the applications, send them off to Washington, and wait to see if they were selected. Many were commissioned, which I would do in my office. Then I hoped they completed their eight-week orientation at Newport. The quotas increased.

Time was moving on. Vietnam continued, along with the wounded. I needed help. The Army and Air Force nurse recruiters had smaller areas to cover than I had. Another nurse was sent to help me. She would be there several months, but then she would be released from the Navy. She was a lieutenant from Massachusetts and had come from Da Nang. Good news. The office was also assigned a new line officer, a lieutenant, but she was not involved with nursing.

The two new female officers wanted to live in Boston, so they found an apartment complex but discovered that they could not afford it. They wanted me to join them so we could all share the rent. From that location, we would be able to walk to work. It was a complex for young professionals. Maybe I did need a change, and it would be closer to work. However, I had my furniture.

They said, "No problem! We will make it fit."

Three LTs, all Navy officers: a blond, a brunette, and a redhead. More trouble for the CO.

I moved, and since I was senior, I had the largest room for a lot of my things.

My back had been giving me problems again, and I ended up flat on my back in traction. I had about two weeks to give the new nurse a crash course. Since she had been a Nurse Corps candidate, she was familiar with many of the forms.

This time, I had a phone in my room so I could talk to the office, and again papers were brought to me for signature. I also bought a TV for my room and had it installed near the ceiling so I could see it.

I was getting close to my three years and orders. My back would not take much more driving. I wanted to work in a hospital, not be a patient. Vietnam was paying me back.

* * *

Soon, I received my orders. I was ready. I could not complain. I would finish my three-year assignment in Boston and I was being assigned to the Naval Hospital Oakland, California, near San Francisco. It was a large teaching hospital, and it was also receiving patients from Vietnam. I knew it would be very busy. California would be a new state for me. I had a month left in Boston.

On my last trip to the Naval Hospital Chelsea, I stopped by the ICU to tell them I would be leaving, since they had all checked in on me while I was a patient there. One of the nurses, Doris, asked if I was driving out to California alone, and I said yes. No one thought this was a good idea with my back. Then she said that if I wanted some company, she would come with me.

Doris said she would like to stop in San Diego so we could spend a day or two visiting with her friends, who were Vietnam nurses. Then she would come to Oakland with me and fly back to Boston. She did not have enough money to fly both ways. I took her up on her offer, and she said that she also had a friend who was stationed at Oakland. This was also good news to me, since I knew no one out there.

While I was still in Boston, another nurse, who was named Ann O., reported to recruiting duty. She had just come from Japan and would be working in Boston for several months as she waited for her next assignment, the Navy Nurse Practitioner Program in San Diego. We agreed to put her up in our apartment in Boston until she moved west. She could have my room when I left, and then maybe whoever came to replace me at the office might move in.

It was time to pack again, and I was looking forward to getting back to a hospital. I would miss certain aspects of recruiting, especially talking with the young nurses. I wondered, *"How many will I see on active duty? How many will be stationed with me?"*

Chapter 38

Naval Hospital
Oakland, California
1970–1974

My trip started across country to my new duty station: Naval Hospital Oakland, California. Doris, the nurse who had worked in the ICU at Naval Hospital Chelsea, Massachusetts, was with me, and it was good to have company for this long trip. Good times were shared as we talked about the Navy and Vietnam and stopped to see a few sights along the way. We made it to the Western states, and then we decided to stop at a motel one evening around 10:00 P.M.

I had a shower, washed my hair, and hopped into bed. Doris was next, and she said she would set the alarm clock for 6:00 A.M. We were both eager to make it to San Diego as quickly as possible so we could visit with her Vietnam nurse friends and see a little of San Diego before I headed North to Oakland.

The alarm went off, and I woke first and dressed. My hair was still wet, and I thought, *"It should be dry by now."*

Doris got up next. Then we packed the car, left the key in the motel's drop box, and returned to the parking lot.

It was still dark. The parking lot was quiet, and I suddenly thought, *"There is no activity. Some people should be leaving by now."*

I did not have my watch on, so Doris looked at hers. She said, "My watch must have stopped. It shows midnight."

"It can't be," I said. "I'll turn the car on and check the time."

It *was* midnight; we had slept one hour. Now what? The entire motel did not have any lights on. All were asleep. Our key could not be retrieved from its spot in the drop box. So, we decided to leave.

Three hours later, we both needed coffee. The only place open was a truckers' stop; we were in the middle of nowhere. Did we want to stop here? Not really, but we wanted the coffee. We both needed to stay awake.

When we entered the diner, all the men stopped talking and looked at us. We took a booth. The waitress came, took our order, and wanted to know where we were headed. Apparently, the men were all asking her about us. I guess we looked a little out of place.

One of the truckers, kidding around, said, "You two must be going to San Diego to see your boyfriends in the Navy." I think the waitress had heard us talking about San Diego.

We laughed and said, "We *are* Navy."

They were curious about what we did. We said, "Nurses."

Since this was 1970 and the Vietnam War continued, one asked if we had been overseas. We both said, "Yes, Vietnam."

Now the entire diner was interested in the conversation, and many of the men had questions. One man asked if we had seen combat. Doris told him that we both had, adding that I had a Purple Heart. Soon they were all talking about Vietnam. Then they paid for our breakfast, thanking us for our service.

Before we left, I took the map out and started looking at it. I asked them, "What's the best road to take next?"

One said he was leaving soon. He suggested we follow him, and he promised to flash his lights and blow his horn to indicate where I needed to turn. Another trucker said he'd drive behind us and also make sure I took the right turn.

They did not want us to get lost on this lonely road, and they did make sure we took the right turn. After that, I drove a few more hours and then we stopped for some sleep.

It was certainly an interesting night, sitting in a diner full of all truckers.

* * *

Late the next afternoon, we made it to San Diego. We met some nurses at the O Club, and the next morning we took a tour of San Diego and the zoo. The next night and the following day we did more sightseeing and visited more nurses. Then we drove to Oakland and met Sandy Lindelof, who lived outside Oakland. Sandy was a nurse who had been stationed on the hospital ship *AH Repose* (the other ship was *AH Sanctuary*). The ships alternated off the coast of South Vietnam but did not come online till after I returned to the States.

We stayed overnight with Sandy, and then the following morning I took Doris to the airport for her flight back to Boston. I was very thankful that Doris had taken leave and was with me on the long drive. We were also both pleased that we had been able to meet other Vietnam nurses. I would meet up with some of them again.

After I left the airport, I returned to Sandy's place and changed into my uniform. Off to the Naval Hospital. I stopped at the front desk and told them I was reporting for duty. My name was entered into the hospital log, and I was told to go to the personnel office with my record.

The personnel officer came to meet me and congratulated me. As I had been driving cross country, the promotion list was released. My name was on the list for Lieutenant Commander (LCDR). Maybe all the work in Boston helped.

I then met the chief nurse, Captain Sue Smoker, Nurse Corps, United States Navy. The captain said she would pin my new rank insignia, Lieutenant Commander, on my uniform the next day. Great news. I couldn't wait to tell my family.

I learned that I would be the charge nurse of the Medical Intensive Care Unit (MICU). I was not exactly thrilled with that. I had been out of nursing for three years, plus two at a quiet hospital. There had been many changes in nursing, and I had to catch up quickly. Because of my rank, I would be taking the position of the LT who was the current charge nurse. She had just reported in about four months before, and now she had to switch jobs. I felt bad about that, but it happens. Rank takes precedence. It would happen to me later.

* * *

My first task outside of the hospital was to find a place to live. Sandy was a big help and showed me around the area. I knew one thing for certain: I wanted to live close to the hospital. No long drives. The hospital had a list of available apartments close by, and I noticed that one of the addresses on the list seemed to be very close. No price was listed, so I decided to check it out after work.

The road was right behind the hospital up on a hill. I had the street number and phone number but decided I would drive by before calling. It was five minutes from the hospital, and it looked interesting: a new building that was the last one on the street, with a fire trail to the hills beyond. I decided to see if it was possible to look at it now, so I stopped and rang the bell.

An older woman, under five feet, came to the door, and I asked about the apartment. Her name was Polly. I was in my nurse's uniform, and I told her I had just moved from the East Coast to work

Oakland Naval Hospital

at the Navy hospital.

Polly explained that she and her husband, Jack, were the owners; they also lived in one of the apartments. There were five apartments, a courtyard, and a studio. The vacant apartment was over the garage.

I looked at it. It was new and included the entire floor over the garage. There was a kitchen, den, bedroom, bath, living room, and small balcony. The bedroom window overlooked the Oakland Bay Bridge: I would see all the lights in the evening. San Francisco was thirty minutes away. Polly said that deer came down to eat off the bushes.

Everything seemed perfect—except the price. It was out of my range, and I knew it the minute I saw it. I thought, *"Why am I still talking to this woman about the East Coast, Vietnam, and my new job?"* I should have been long gone.

Jack came home from work and joined the conversation. He was in sales and worked as a consultant for a big machinery company, which involved traveling around the country. I mentioned my Vietnam and Boston assignments and explained that I was from a small city in New Hampshire. He said he knew it well, as he had been there several times.

Eventually I checked the time and said that I needed to leave. Polly told her husband that I had looked at the apartment but could not afford it. She told me to take another look at it because she wanted to talk to her husband.

I knew they were going to discuss the price, but I was certain that I still would not be able to afford it. When I came back down, they quoted another price that was closer to my budget, but I still could not do it. The husband asked what I could pay, and I told him what my salary was. (It was government, and anyone could check it.) They lowered the price again. I did not feel comfortable accepting at first, but then they gave me their reasons for doing it.

Polly was alone a good deal, and she felt comfortable with me; the building was professional. There were two married doctors in one apartment, a doctor and nurse in the other, and a schoolteacher in the studio. They said I would fit in and they were not renting the apartments for the money. They had moved from a different area for a change and enjoyed meeting more people.

They had designed the apartments themselves. I knew I certainly could not get anything better or any closer, so I said yes.

I moved in right away but had to buy a living room set. I just could not believe I was so lucky. Their apartment was beautiful, overlooking the hills, and they had a sauna I could use any time. I had been adopted by this couple, and they frequently invited me to dinner. I lived there for four years throughout my stay in Oakland.

* * *

Now to concentrate on my new position. The hospital was very busy, especially the ICUs. They were still receiving casualties from Vietnam. It did not take too long for me to get back into nursing, and my Vietnam experience helped.

I had been there almost a year when the administration officials at the hospital decided to take some of the beds and start a Coronary Care Unit (CCU). The Kaiser Hospital outside San Francisco had a course for nurses going into such units. I went and then helped start this new unit in the back of MICU. I watched patients, taught the nurses and corpsmen, and kept an eye on the interns and residents. We were responsible for cardiac arrests, codes, and resuscitations, along with medications. It was a stressful unit because of the rotation of staff and patients.

Ann O. stopped by to see me on her way to San Diego for the Nurse Practitioner program. She brought me up to date on my previous roommates. One night we both had dates for dinner at the Top of The Mark Restaurant, located in the Mark Hopkins Hotel on Nob Hill in San Francisco (the highest point in downtown SF). We had a wonderful time and enjoyed the view.

* * *

Another year went by. The hospital created a new department: nursing education. It was going to be more formalized and have its own staff. There would be certification and records. Someone needed to teach—a lieutenant commander. A commander would be in charge; they needed an instructor. Would I like the position?

I had to think about it. Teaching was not my specialty. I liked working with corpsmen, but teaching nurses? I was not sure.

Then I thought, *"A move from CCU? A way out. Something new. If it doesn't work, they will move me."* I decided to give it a try.

They found someone for my place, and after her orientation I moved to my new office. It was in the administration wing of the hospital, which was set up like an inverted U. All nursing offices were located on one side; the commanding officer, a rear admiral (RADM), and his aide were in the middle; and on the other side were the offices of the executive officer and the administration staff. My office was the very first one after the closed doors. We were part of the front office, and the admiral walked by my office every day.

I was very busy, and then the commander was pulled for special projects. We were certifying all nurses for CPR (cardiopulmonary resuscitation), isolation technique, and IV therapy (intravenous therapy). They assigned a male LT to the office because we were now teaching the hospital corpsmen.

Each day I listened to the morning and afternoon supervisory reports, so I knew what was happening on the wards; this allowed me to see if they needed more education in certain areas. Then one day the night supervisor was not able to make it to work. They were in a bind and asked if I could do night supervision. My first. Then I did nights, then 3:00 P.M. to 11:00 P.M., and on occasion the day shift. I was added to the rotation schedule. There were several nurses in this rotation group but my primary duties were education.

This was a great experience for me, and I liked doing it. Soon my chief nurse wanted me to go for my master's. This involved a word I did not want to hear—*school.*

She said, "If you want to stay in the Navy and be promoted, you need the degree. Better think about it."

* * *

My apartment was great, and I enjoyed the company of Polly and her husband. They kept me informed on all the places to see. After I had lived there just over two years, Polly suggested I have a party for some of the staff. She liked entertaining and promised to help. I thought a punch would be a good drink because we could prepare it in advance, store it in bottles, and then on the night of the party, we wouldn't need to mix it; we could just pour it into a punch bowl. I said I would make the punch with Polly's recipe (she agreed to supervise), and she said she'd take care of all the appetizers.

All I needed to do was send out the invitations. That was one problem I was very nervous about. Unspoken military protocol meant that the admiral and all the senior people in the administration wing needed to be invited. I was hesitant to invite them, but protocol required it. In the end, I sent the invitations but all the seniors declined. They let the juniors have their party.

The night arrived, and a good group of doctors and nurses came. Polly kept telling me to warn the guests to be very careful on the punch; it tasted like lemonade but it was potent. The Bay Area was in the midst of a heat wave, and everyone was thirsty! The punch bowl was always empty, and they kept asking for more. I don't remember how many times the bowl was refilled. Finally it was midnight; time to leave. Several of them had to work Sunday: ICU, ER, day supervisor, and ward nurses. Some decided they were too tired to drive, so they stayed overnight. They were still talking when I went to bed. The next morning, the couches, love seat, and even the space behind the couch were all occupied.

Then, the phone rang. The night supervisor said four staff had called in sick, including the day supervisor, who had to give report to the Admiral at 9:00 A.M. What had I done to the staff? Some of the doctors made it, but they were not looking well. I thought, *"Am I in trouble now!"* Eventually my overnight guests all left, and I went down to tell Polly how much they had enjoyed her punch. She said, "I told you."

The next morning I was in my office early, and the admiral's aide came by laughing; he had been invited but couldn't come. He had served in Vietnam, and every day he would stop by my office and there would be an update. Now he said the hospital staff all wanted to know when the next party would be. They wanted to be invited.

Later the admiral came by and stopped. He mentioned the party and said he was sorry he had missed it. He was also laughing. Captain Smoker just went by and shook her head. I was glad they thought my party was a success.

* * *

I was enjoying my time in Oakland. I was on the doctor's bowling team, and I had season tickets to the plays in San Francisco, with dinner before in famous restaurants. It was a great place.

I also had lots of company. My mother visited twice a year, and she and Polly played cards and other games when I was working. My sister and aunt and several friends from the East Coast also came. I had a circle of friends at the hospital and on several weekends, there were trips to Hawaii. We would get a hop from one of the planes at NAS Alameda, Alameda, California. We'd leave on Friday and come back Tuesday. We often traveled up and down the coast, and we went to Lake Tahoe, wine country, Yosemite, and Monterey several times. I was able to see all the sights there.

One piece of good news I learned while in Oakland was that my senior nurse in Vietnam, CDR Richman, who had gone back to the states on the medevac, was still alive and on oxygen. She had friends in California and came for a visit. We continued to keep in touch.

One time when my mother was visiting and I was working 3:00 P.M. to 11:00 P.M., a commander down the street decided to come and take my mother to one of the weekly bingo games for senior nurses, captains, and commanders at the O Club. I could not believe this: my mother was with all my senior officers! She came back with all the items she had won. She had a great time, won a bunch of very nice prizes (no cash was ever awarded), and couldn't wait to repeat the experience. They did take her again, and she was always lucky.

* * *

I also heard about graduate school again from both my mother and the captain. I enrolled in a class at one of the colleges, which was a shock to my brain. Then I looked into what I would need for grad school. Oh, that awful subject—statistics—could I face it? The only place I could take it was an evening class at the University of California, Berkley. I enrolled. In order to take the class, I had to drive through Berkley and pass all the students demonstrating against the war on the four corners of a busy intersection downtown. I hoped the light would quickly turn green before anyone had time to see my car sticker.

In class I was in over my head. Midterm exam was coming up. We were all told if we missed the exam, we would fail the course. I went, but I was not ready for the exam. And guess what?

Someone called in a bomb scare, and we all had to leave the building. I waited about fifteen minutes and then thought they would cancel the classes, so I left and drove home. At the next class, the student beside me asked why I hadn't stayed to take the exam. They had waited and gone back in.

The professor just looked at me throughout the class. Afterwards I had to explain why I had left. What else: blame it on Vietnam and the bombs over there. I told him I knew I was not doing well but I really needed to pass. I did pass, but what a headache.

Next I put my applications in for graduate school. Then I had to wait to see if I would be accepted at a school and if the Navy selection board would approve my request to pursue the degree.

* * *

I was kept very busy with new staff coming aboard, updates, and special projects for nursing service in the hospital. One day, we received word that our Vietnam POWs were going to be released from North Vietnam. Oakland was going to be one of the receiving hospitals on the West Coast. This was called "Operation Home-coming," and the returning POWs were called *repatriates*. A ward was set aside for them. They would be together, they would have privacy from staff and reporters, and security would check people going in. The repatriates could leave when they wanted. The hospital staff was excited. When would they arrive?

After the repatriates were released, they flew to Clark Air Force Base Hospital in the Philippines for medical evaluations. They were debriefed, received new uniforms, and made calls to their families. A brief stop was scheduled for Hawaii, and then for those who were stable, the next stop would be closer to their homes and medical facilities for treatment. Oakland would be receiving several. Their planes would land at Travis Air Force Base outside San Francisco on different days, and the repatriates would be brought to the hospital.

Ambulances and buses were sent to bring them back. Each vehicle going out to meet them had nurses and hospital corpsmen to accompany them back to the hospital. Patients heading to the ICU had an ICU nurse in the ambulance.

I had told my captain that if they needed an escort on short notice I would like to go, since I was in Vietnam when the first Navy pilot was shot down on August 5, 1964. It would be like a closure on my Vietnam days. However, this seemed unlikely. Most of the nurses chosen for this duty were young ones.

Since I was in the administration wing, I knew from the aide when the planes were coming. Eventually, there were only two more planes expected. On next to the last day, nothing was said to me. Well, I was senior; this was really for the ensigns and lieutenant junior grades.

The morning of February 16, 1973, the aide stopped by and said, "It's going to be a good day today."

Later the admiral went by. He had a big smile and said, "Good day coming up."

Then the captain stopped and said, "I want to see you after morning report."

I thought, *"What now?"* At 9:00 A.M. I reported to her office and was told that at 9:30 A.M. I was to report to an office around the corner to receive my instructions.

I was going to Travis Air Force Base to meet the plane that LCDR Everett Alvarez was on, and a brief ceremony would take place. He was the pilot who was shot down when I was in Vietnam. I was excited! I would ride out in the hospital sedan and escort him back. Once the plane landed, all the other repatriates returning would deplane and come back on buses or ambulances.

LCDR Alvarez came down the steps and was greeted by the Commanding Officer of the Base and escorted to the podium. A crowd of 600 people were waiting, and there were cheers. He had spent eight and a half years as a POW.

LCDR Alvarez spoke for a short time, and when he was finished, I went over and escorted him to the car, and then we were driven back to the hospital. I had to tell him that a smaller group of two hundred people—family, neighbors, and hospital staff—would also be there to greet him at the hospital. On the way back I told him I had been in Vietnam when his plane was shot down.

When we reached the hospital, I escorted LCDR Alvarez down a cordoned-off lane and brought him to Rear Admiral Faucett, Commanding Officer of the Hospital. I would not see him again, so I gave him a kiss on the cheek as a welcome back and best wishes. I didn't know that picture would be on the front page in the *Oakland Tribune* the next day.

I had received my orders on Christmas Eve, 1963, to Vietnam, and to me this was the war's end, 1973. The fighting force left Vietnam, but the official end was two years later, April 1975.

* * *

I continued working in education and taking my turns in supervision in the hospital. I received my acceptance for graduate school at California State University, Fresno. My next assignment was DUINS (Duty Under Instruction) Fresno, for my master's degree in Nursing Administration, starting in the fall.

I had to tell Polly and her husband I would be leaving. It was definite now. Both were very upset, but they had known such a time would come. Four years had been my longest assignment, and they knew I had requested graduate school.

Polly, who usually drank a bit, seemed to be doing more. One Saturday afternoon, her husband, Jack, called me. He said he could not wake Polly and asked me to come down. I went right down and when I opened the door, I could not see well; their apartment was full of smoke. Jack seemed unsteady but was walking toward the bedroom.

I noticed Polly sitting up on the couch in the den. I rushed over to her and sat down. She was wrapped in her afghan. I was going to check for a pulse, but when I moved flames came through the afghan. Now the couch was in flames on the other side. I grabbed Polly and carried her outside in the courtyard, yelling, "Help! Fire!"

Help came from upstairs, and we put the fire on her out and closed the door to the apartment so no more air would get in. The fire department came, and they brought Jack out. He had fallen asleep.

I had to do CPR. When the ambulance arrived, I went with them to the civilian hospital. We tried starting an IV in the ambulance, but going so fast over the hills made it very difficult. She died a few minutes after we arrived at the ER. The only place she was not burned was her face and neck.

Polly had been a heavy smoker, and with her drinking, I believe the cigarette dropped into the afghan and smoldered for a length of time. I had always feared something like this would happen and had talked to both of them about the potentially deadly combination of alcohol and cigarettes.

The hospital staff told me that Jack was on his way, so I waited till he arrived at the ER and was notified. Then, the rest of the family in Southern California came. I knew they would have difficult days ahead.

Another death, and the smell of smoke. I had seen too many in Vietnam. Since I would be leaving in three weeks, I decided to spend my last days at the home of Pat Clancy, another Navy nurse, and just move my furniture south to Fresno. It would have been too difficult to look down at their apartment every day and remember all the good times I had shared there.

Chapter 39

Graduate School
California State University, Fresno
1974–1975

After I received my orders, I made a trip to Fresno to look for an apartment. I found one on the main street going to the campus. It was about two miles away, but straight driving. It was in a large apartment building, and my apartment looked at a side street from a little balcony. The street was quiet and had a lot of trees with a good place to sit and study. The rents were reasonable, so I signed a lease for a two-bedroom apartment, which was located over the one where the managers, a married couple, lived. I paid for a month in advance to hold it, and I let them know that I would be there for a year and a half. I hoped to finish grad school in that time.

I moved my things to the apartment early because of the fire in Oakland. Then I went back to Oakland, completed my time, returned to Fresno, and settled in.

I started classes and hit the books, as they say. I was so afraid I would not do well; I felt extra pressure because the Navy was paying for everything, including my salary. I was going for a master's, and my major was Nursing Administration. However, I also had to take clinical courses.

I thought, *"Something different."* I decided to try psychology/ mental health. I thought, *"Maybe this would be good—working with people."* I needed the okay from my advisor, and I also had to write a thesis. On what? This would be a problem. Fortunately, we had a little time to think about that and get that approval. My classes were small, which made it good for discussions.

The first week I met the dean, who would teach several of our courses. I also met the other professors and my classmates. Two of these were former Navy nurses. I only had one class with each, but it was nice to know that they were around. They were still working, so I was very lucky.

It was class and study! Then the dean invited any student who wanted to go with her to attend conferences and workshops in the state. These were held on weekends for the senior nurses in Management or Education. Participants had to pay the registration fee, which was a little expensive ($150 to $250). The dean did the driving and split the room cost. Several of these topics sounded interesting and I was curious to learn what other hospitals were doing, but I first waited to see if anyone else would volunteer.

No one did, so I said I'd like to go.

Then the dean asked, "Do you like dogs?"

I said, "Yes."

She explained that she always took her dog with her. She had a miniature schnauzer. She said, "You should come over the night before, so the dog can meet you."

Shortly after we started the four-hour drive, the dog acted up in the back seat. I did not know what was wrong. The dean said, "The dog always rides in the front seat."

I had a decision to make. I thought, *"This is the dean's dog. Should I sit in the back, or should I bring the dog up front with me?"*

The dog came up front, sat in my lap, and eventually went to sleep. I thought, *"This should get me an A!"* It was a cute dog.

We checked in, she took the dog out, and we went to a couple of lectures. Then we attended the social hour, followed by dinner. It was an interesting evening, and I met many of the top nursing administrators in the state. That night the dog decided to sleep with me. Now I was in trouble. The dog never did this. I thought, *"There goes my A!"*

The next morning, we attended lectures till 1:00 P.M. and then returned to Fresno. The dog was on my lap during the ride back. I later learned that other students didn't attend these workshops because some were working, it was too expensive, or they didn't like dogs.

* * *

My mother came for a short visit, but I was busy with exams. I did take her to Las Vegas, plus some other areas. She liked to travel. I spent holidays with one former Navy nurse and her family. When the end of the Vietnam War was announced in April 1975, the three Navy nurses met and celebrated. I also had a few trips back to Oakland to see friends there.

My classes continued, and I attended a couple more seminars with the dean and her dog. I had to start work on my thesis, and most of my time I was involved with that. When it came to statistics, I needed help! One of the professors who taught the subject helped me. I also made contact by mail with a group of Navy nurses as a study group.

Eventually, we each had to make arrangements to shadow a director of nursing in her position for two weeks. I planned to choose Naval Hospital Oakland but learned that I could not select a place I had been before. The other nurses were requesting hospitals around where they lived. I thought, *"I might as well try for something big."* I decided on one of the very large hospitals in San Francisco.

I had two in mind. I had met the directors at the conferences I had gone to with my Dean of Nursing. I sent one a letter requesting this. I received an affirmative answer and now had to find a place to stay. My first choice was the BOQ at Treasure Island, Naval Base, California. This was a small Navy facility underneath the Oakland Bay Bridge, and there were a few rooms available to request for a short time. I called and reserved one for my dates. I needed the final approval from the school and explained that I would be with the assistant director part of the time. My professor was surprised I had requested that size of a hospital.

From Treasure Island, I just took the ramp onto the bridge and then drove to the hospital. I arrived there very early, which meant I could find a close parking spot. It was my routine for two weeks, and they had a schedule for me. I couldn't believe I was able to do this. I spent a wonderful two weeks observing in this famous city.

Since I was taking psychology and mental health, I also sat in on some of the group sessions at the VA Hospital in Fresno. This allowed me to become familiar with some of the assistance that was available to veterans, and consequently I was able to help steer my landlady to them. Her husband, a veteran, was showing symptoms requiring assistance.

Time was getting closer to finish my thesis and take final exams. My grades were good. I made it: a Master's in Nursing (MSN). The actual graduation ceremony would not be for several months. They asked, "Will you return?"

No. They would need to mail my degree to me. Now I belonged to the Navy again. Well, I always did. I wondered, *"Where will my next assignment be?"*

I knew they would assign me where I was needed.

Chapter 40

Naval Hospital
Lemoore, California
1975

I now had my new assignment, a small hospital at the naval air station (NAS) in Lemoore, California, which was located a little over an hour's drive from Fresno. NAS Lemoore is a base for training and operational squadrons in the San Joaquin Valley, in Central California. The operational squadrons were assigned to the carriers when they left on deployments, and these were attack squadrons, ready for any conflict. Training squadrons remained at NAS Lemoore. The families were at Lemoore.

I couldn't say I was very happy about the orders, because I had hoped for a larger hospital. However, the Nurse Corps usually had a reason for its decisions, and I bet that their reason was to save the cost of moving me. They had paid my tuition and salary while I was getting my master's degree. Now they would not have to pay for a long-distance move, and I was obligated to accept their decision.

This would be my second naval air station. I had enjoyed NAS Pensacola, Florida, so I hoped for the best. It was isolated, so I decided to go check about housing. Most of the families were living on base or in Lemoore. There was a BOQ, but I didn't want that. Since I didn't know any nurses there, I decided to check with the chief nurse, who was a commander, and ask for her advice before I made any decisions.

I made an appointment to see the chief nurse, and she gave me some suggestions. I also learned that she was retiring in about four months and another commander had orders to be her relief. The new commander was coming from the East Coast. Since I was reporting with my degree in nursing administration, the current commander would orient me to the office duties and then I could take them until her relief reported. The current commander would be there to help and answer any questions. Then there would be a few weeks when I would be on my own. This sounded great to me.

I rented a new townhouse in Lemoore. It was a nice place. However, after several months and an extremely high electric bill, I discovered that my meter and my neighbors' meter were reversed. The city could not correct the bills. Since I was single and they were a family of four, the charges weren't similar, and I moved out to an area that had several ground-floor apartments in a row. There was a small pool in back and no problem with the electricity.

When I reported for duty, I met the commanding officer and others in administration. I quickly became familiar with the staff and the layout of the hospital; the inpatient was small but active, and the clinics were busy. It did not take me too long to know most of the routines and reports

I was being trained to be the assistant. However, when the new commander reported, it turned out that she had been the operating room supervisor in a large hospital on the East Coast, and she decided she did not need an assistant or help on routines. Consequently, I was moved to the outpatient clinic.

When you are junior in rank, you can expect changes. I always found changes interesting because I continued to learn. The commander changed some of the routines and paperwork for the commanding officer, and he was not pleased. He told her to check with me on the way he wanted things done. A couple of times a day, I would hear my name over the PA system to report to the nursing office so I could explain his preference. If I was in the clinics and did not hear my name over the PA, which did not work in all of the rooms, then the commander would come to find me. I was an LCDR caught in the middle. Things were not going well.

Then some of the young nurse ensigns and lieutenant junior grades had some difficulties. They wanted out. The recruiter in me felt compelled to help. We were a distance from a lot of extra activities. I asked them, "Have you been to the Officers' Club?" They said no, so I took them to the Officers' Club and happy hour to meet others from the base. They did, and later there were engagements and weddings and return to civilian life. I was very happy for them. Now I had gifts to buy and weddings to attend.

I—along with some pilots and medical personnel—bought several acres of land in the state of Washington. A new land development was planned. (All looked good until Mount Saint Helens erupted in the 1980s, which ended the development plans.) My acres were mostly pine trees with a stream going through it. I no longer own that now.

Soon I experienced health problems. It was my back again. X-rays were done and I was told that nothing was wrong. I was on medication. I could not stand the pain and went to the MD again and said I wanted a consult. He decided to do another X-ray. The results showed that I had cervical discs pinching off some nerves. At least I knew it was not in my mind. I needed neurosurgery. Where did I want to go? I had the choice of San Diego or Oakland.

I decided on Oakland since I still had friends there. I went up there for more tests. Surgery was scheduled, and I would be out a month. The commander was not happy. The chief of neurosurgery told me it was from my injury in Vietnam. I drove back to Lemoore to make some arrangements and pack a suitcase. Then I was driven back to Oakland. The surgery was done, but they could only do one level. The other would need to be done later.

I recuperated at Oakland. I then returned to Lemoore, but I was in a neck brace, so my mother flew out to visit. Later I developed a complication and had to return to Oakland for more care. Bernie Majewski, one of the nurses, spent some of her free time with my mother and, when I was working, checked on her. She lived just a few doors away. One of the reasons my mother loved to visit my duty stations was the time she spent with the other nurses and the opportunities she had to hear about their experiences.

Finally, I was back to duty, and I was assigned to the operating room. This required a specialty code—more training—which I did not have, and I only had on-the-job training in Vietnam. I had disliked my time in the OR since my short time as a student and had gotten more than my share of the OR in Vietnam. In Lemoore, the rooms were very cold, and I had to wear double clothing. It was not a good place for me.

* * *

One Monday, I went to work and received a message to report to the commanding officer's office. I had noticed the chief nurse was not at work. The commanding officer informed me that she was gone for two weeks and I was to cover the nursing department while she was away. I was annoyed. They both must have known this would be happening.

"Where did she go?" I asked.

He said, "I am not to tell you."

I thought, *"Selection board time. People disappear."*

Selection boards are held to select officers for promotion. Officers are evaluated on training, experience, and performance.

Members of the board must meet certain criteria. There are other requirements that need to be met also.

I then said, "Washington?"

He said, "Well, she is there now, yes."

I said, "She is sitting on my board for commander."

He nodded his head.

I thought, *"I don't think I will make it."*

She returned. More weeks went by. A long wait. Finally, I was told to report to the CO's office.

I thought, *"Is the list out?*

He told me to have a seat. He said, "I have been talking to Washington. The list was released, and you are on it. You have made commander."

Official paperwork would be coming. I told him that when I had the CDR insignia placed on my uniform, I wanted him and my chief nurse to do the honors.

Once I had my new insignia on my uniform, I wrote a letter to the Navy Nurse Corps Division in Washington and requested orders to the East Coast. I specifically asked for a large hospital.

I learned that I would need to wait a little longer. They had cut back on cross-country moves. I had been seeing my father on my trips back East, but before I was transferred my father came out to visit me. I then took him around to see some of the sights in California.

* * *

One night I was on call for the OR and was waiting with the staff. We were on alert in case we needed to do a C-section (cesarean section), but it was still possible that the patient could deliver on her own. I was sitting with the OB doctor and the pediatrician in the break room after midnight. Then things changed. There were two other women who were getting close to delivering. I thought, *"What if the three are ready at the same time? We would each be delivering a baby."*

The OB nurse came out to tell us the current status. The MD went to check them. All were going to deliver at the same time. He delivered one, the OB nurse had one, and I had one. The pediatrician had a busy night also. All were healthy. That night we had a happy ending.

Another time, I was at home when I got an OR call after midnight. Two planes, returning from the south, had been lost on radar. They thought the planes had crashed; the Tule Fog, a thick ground fog that settles in the San Joaquin Valley and Sacramento Valley, was extremely dense. These were not military planes, but the pilots were. Two young officers: a LT and the LTjg who was a male nurse on our staff.

This was just a call to alert me, but I said, "I'm coming in." I had a ten-mile drive. The fog was so thick I had to drive with my door open so I could see the white line on the other side of the road and avoid the ditch.

I didn't think I would make it, and if another car had approached from the opposite direction, I am not sure what would have happened. I did not realize the fog was that bad until I was a distance from Lemoore. There was no place to turn around. I made it, but it was a stressful drive.

Many of the staff were there, all waiting for news. The base personnel had teams out searching, and we waited!

Eventually we were notified that they found one plane and were bringing someone back. Alive? Name? Not our nurse. This pilot was alive with broken bones, and he was brought in for treatment. The wait continued. An hour went by. The plane was found but they were still searching. Not a good sign. Then the final call. The body was found. I called the CDR. The day staff would be coming soon. He was a good nurse. It hit home for many.

It took several months for the staff to get over this. For me, it was another reminder of how quickly death can sneak up. I thought of the young men in Vietnam and the plane crashes there.

* * *

Several months went by, and then I was finally called about orders. I was told it would be a while longer. Eventually I received orders to the Naval Regional Medical Center, Portsmouth, Virginia. I was pleased with those orders. It was the largest hospital on the East Coast except Bethesda. I did not want Washington.

I knew very little about Virginia. Would I miss Lemoore? I didn't think so. It was the least favorable duty station, although I did learn more about the clinics and the OR. In California, I had also enjoyed my time at Naval Hospital Oakland, earned my MSN degree in administration, and made good friends. We still keep in touch today.

I was excited about the chance to move back to the East Coast after eight years in California. I let my family know. Now to pack up and fly home.

Chapter 41

Naval Regional Medical Center Portsmouth, Virginia January 1978–January 1982

I decided to have my car driven back to New Hampshire for me, to save my back. I spent one week's leave there and then drove down to Virginia. Nancy, one of the nurses whom I had been stationed with in Portsmouth, New Hampshire, had invited me to stay with her in Virginia until I was settled. She was a commander who was assigned as the operating room supervisor at the Naval hospital.

I had a tour of the hospital grounds. Naval Regional Medical Center had two large buildings. The smaller one was old and had a part in history. This was called Building 1, and it was near the water. Their patients were obstetrics, delivery, nursery, pediatrics, and psychiatry. The newer one had several floors and all the other patients. There were also many smaller buildings.

I was now anxious to see the housing areas as I had decided to buy a house instead of renting. I would be there four years. I heard that many of the nurses lived in the Virginia Beach section, but they had to face the tunnel every day and a lot of traffic. I was not interested in that.

After looking around for a few days, I decided on a brick ranch in a new development in Chesapeake, Virginia. It was right over the Portsmouth line and not that far from the hospital. The house was not completed, so I was able to pick the paint, wallpaper, and some other items. In three weeks, I was able to move in. My first house.

Naval Hospital, Portsmouth, Virginia

There was still a lot to do, but I had my very own place.

I had written my letter to the director of nursing services, a Navy captain (previous title was chief nurse), and stated when I would report for duty. I was eager to learn where I would be assigned. I was told there were three other captains there and several commanders who had the title of patient care coordinators (supervisors) with many more duties. This was a very active hospital with all specialties. I hoped I would be assigned to an area I liked.

I checked in with my records and brought them to the personnel office; they sent me on to meet the assistant director, a captain. She seemed very nice. I later learned she had been recalled to active duty after Korea, and she had been assigned to a hospital ship during Vietnam. Many years after we both retired, we would see each other at Military Officers Association of America (MOAA) meetings.

My next meeting was with the director; that was very different. She seemed annoyed that I was there and wanted to know how I had received orders cross-country. One of her nurses had been trying to go west with no success. I was given my assignment, but she made it clear that she wasn't sure I could handle it. I was a little annoyed but said nothing. I had never heard of her before, although she was a very senior captain.

My assignment was a very busy area. I had three floors: 6, 7, and 8. Floor 6 had two surgical enlisted wards; 7 was a medical enlisted ward, and 8 had the Medical Intensive Care Unit (MICU) and a Coronary Care Unit (CCU). I was lucky—but she didn't know that. I had all military nurses and hospital corpsmen for my staff. My office was on the eighth floor, and I shared it with another coordinator.

I had to do the staffing for all areas. That was not a problem because I had been doing it before, but I asked if there was a pattern that they used. I was told to do it any way I would like, so I did it the same way as the schedule in Oakland and Lemoore, which was quite common.

Usually when a nurse started a new position, the assistant took care of any problems or differences that arose as they learned the routine. I was sent to the Director.

She called me into her office and told me I didn't know anything about scheduling. I changed my method to please her, but later she changed it. This became our pattern: she told me to do something one way, and then two weeks later she told me to do it another way. I spoke to a couple of coordinators and learned this happened on occasion. They also urged me to wait because she was scheduled to retire in six months.

My primary responsibility was to ensure all the patients received outstanding care, utilizing all the staff and tools available. They were young nurses and hospital corpsmen and needed education. It was a demanding area and the time went by quickly.

* * *

After I was settled in my house I decided to do some landscaping. I had a large, open space with fields behind the house, and I wanted to put up a fence. I went to Sears and looked at the different types of wood. I decided on a cedar fence instead of pine. The cedar was more expensive, but I wanted it anyway. I paid for it and requested that they call me before installing it because I wanted to be there. Instead, I came home from work one day and there was the fence.

I went out and checked it and found they had installed a pine fence instead of a cedar fence. It was a large area. I went to Sears to complain, explaining that I did not want the pine fence. The Sears people told me I had to deal with the subcontractor. Getting in touch with the subcontractor was difficult to do; then the subcontractor refused to take it down. I spent more time going back and forth between the two, and then someone at the hospital suggested I take them to small claims court. I made a claim against Sears as they had my money.

It was a new experience. I filled out the paperwork and received a court date. Meanwhile, I collected all the documentation. My court date arrived, and I went to work for a few hours; then off to court. I was in my Navy uniform. I found a seat in the middle of the room, and while I was waiting, three sailors came in and sat behind me. I presented my case, and then came the person from Sears.

The judge looked at my ribbons and asked if I had received a Purple Heart.

I said, "Yes sir."

He said, "Where?"

I said "Nurse, Vietnam."

Then we returned to court business, and he asked me what I wanted.

I said, "I want the fence down this afternoon and the correct fence replaced."

He ruled that the fence would be taken down that day and replaced the next day. My case was over.

I walked by the sailors, and they said, "Go Navy!"

When I returned from the hospital, the fence was gone. Later I spent many hours planting trees along the fence.

* * *

The new director of nursing services was Captain Mary Nielubowicz; she reported from the Bureau of Medicine and Surgery (BUMED) in the Navy Nurse Corps Division (Washington). She had been my detailer (the person who made all the nurse corps assignments to Naval medical facilities). She was a "people person"—what a difference!

She asked all the coordinators if we would like to change areas. We all said no; we were used to our areas.

I started training my charge nurses on some of my duties so that if I was not on duty, they could assume some of the work. It was good experience for them, although any time that I had to be absent, another commander was still responsible for the area. All the commanders met in the morning, and if anyone needed extra help, we took care of it. We all helped each other. It was a good group.

I did have a few roadblocks over the years. I developed a DVT (deep vein thrombosis) in my leg and was admitted to the hospital and placed on Heparin. I was finally discharged, and my mother came to see me. Three days after she arrived my sister called: my father had died. We both flew back to New Hampshire, and I arranged for the funeral.

Then it was back to Virginia. The next year was busy with a lot of company and work. Then I received another call from my sister: my mother was in the hospital. We were told it was her gallbladder. I returned to New Hampshire again and spent a lot of time with her. One night I asked the nurse to see her chart. I looked at her EKG and noticed she had had a heart attack.

My coronary care experience in Oakland was very helpful. I spoke with the doctor in the morning but he did not know this had occurred; he had not looked at the EKG. The heart attack was a bad one, and she had not received any treatment. I had my sister and aunt come to see her. My mother died as I was taking my aunt back to her house.

I was more than a little upset; she was only seventy-one years old. I had another funeral to plan, and then I needed to return to Virginia. The nursing department was very understanding.

* * *

My office was in an excellent spot, I could look out the window and watch the aircraft carrier and the escort ships leave, going on deployments and returning to homeport. Sometimes I took a junior nurse to walk over to Building 1 at lunchtime, and then we were very close to the ships. The sailors manned the rail as they passed by the hospital, which was an impressive sight.

My third year I had a new office mate, Commander Ruth Purinton, who was also from New Hampshire. She also had been in Vietnam and had just completed her master's. We would often share our experiences. We also covered each other's area if one of us had to be away. We became good friends, and to this date, we continue to make weekly phone calls. She retired in Virginia. There were many places to see in Virginia and the surrounding states. Holidays in Williamsburg, Virginia, were always a favorite. Several nurses on the Portsmouth side frequently planned a function or travel to the Virginia Beach side. CDR Sandy Lindelof was one of these nurses. I had stayed with her when I first arrived in Oakland, and we remain in contact. Her home now is North Carolina. I became friends with several other nurses too; Christmas cards bring us up to date.

During my third year, I decided to take a trip to Ireland with my aunt. I had always wanted to see the country my mother had been to when she heard the name Darby, my middle name. We traveled with a small group and had a wonderful time.

I also had orders and was sent to Washington for selection boards for Commanders and Lieutenant Commanders. I was there for two weeks for the rank in session These were difficult to do, as not everyone is selected for promotion. I also attended some conferences and workshops, so I was getting to know Washington.

* * *

One experience I'll never forget occurred when a blizzard was predicted. All the ships left port. Virginia and the Coast were not really prepared for snow. Everyone was talking about it: When would it start? How many inches? I had weekend duty: 7:00 A.M. to 3:00 A.M. I was the senior nurse and responsible for all nursing issues in the hospital. I went home on Saturday around 5:00 P.M. as I had stayed longer to go over potential staffing problems with the 3:00 P.M. to 11:00 P.M. nurse. It did not begin to snow until about 10:00 P.M.

I received a call that the night nurses from Virginia Beach had started calling to say they could not make it. Portsmouth only had a few flakes. The hospital called me, and I asked them to keep the military nurses there. I also instructed them to ask the civilian nurses to stay if possible; we could not order them. Some stayed, while others had to leave to take care of their families. Later I called the hospital to tell them I would be coming in.

I had packed a bag and prepared to return to the hospital, but I didn't rush because there was still very little snow. I also wanted the two lieutenants to have some experience handling things without me.

I kept checking the windows. Within thirty minutes, it was coming down faster than I had anticipated. I went to my car and realized I could not make it over the bridge. I had waited too long. Now what?

I looked across at my neighbor's house, and his lights came on. I knew the family well. It was close to midnight, so I thought, *"Maybe he is going to work."* He was a police detective for the Portsmouth Police Department. I called and asked, and he said, "Yes. There's an Army truck coming for me and collecting other police."

The police station was very close to the hospital, so I asked if I could get a ride with them.

He said, "I'll get you in."

I put my winter gear back on, and my havelock covered most of my face. The big Army truck arrived and I made it to my neighbor's driveway. At that point, the snow was drifting around and some of the drifts came up to my knees. The truck was full. My neighbor, because of his position, took the front seat. Without mentioning my name, he told the group that I was a Navy officer who needed to get to the hospital. They had to pull me up—it was a very high truck. Since there was no space, I had to sit on one of the men. One of them made a comment about my size, noting that I did not weigh much.

It was a difficult ride in and over the bridge. The roads had not been plowed, and the men were not sure we would make it.

The men started telling ribald jokes, and I realized that they did not know I was a woman. Then my neighbor told them, "Watch it! There's a female back there with you."

They were shocked and embarrassed. I had not spoken before, but now I simply said, "I was in Vietnam." It changed the conversation.

We made it to the entrance of the hospital, but the gates were closed so no one could enter. I had been afraid of that. No one was out plowing, and ambulances were diverted. The men in the truck did not know what to do with me. They offered to take me to the police station. However, I had called the hospital before I left and had been warned this might happen. I had told the staff at the hospital to be on the lookout in case I needed to walk. The Army truck left me at the gate, and I walked the rest of the way.

It was difficult with the wind and the snow. The glass door to the entrance of the hospital was covered in snow; they could not see out. I had to clean it a little. I was covered myself and looked like a snowman. The storm paralyzed the city for three days, and no one could move around. There were very few snowplows.

I was there for that time, along with the rest of the staff. All patients were cared for, the staff was fed, and places were found for them to sleep. No emergencies. We were relieved on the afternoon of the third day, and all was under control. It was one storm I will always remember.

* * *

Another memorable incident occurred when Ruth and I were going to be responsible for two nurses from the Philippine Navy. We had them for two weeks, but they would be in the States for two months so they could observe different aspects of military nursing. A few days before they arrived, Ruth and I heard a loud noise outside our office. Since this was part of my area, I went out to investigate.

Two men from maintenance were removing a refrigerator from the doctors' conference room, which was right next to our office, and replacing it with a new one. The doctors often held conferences during their lunch breaks, and they had used this refrigerator to store their lunches. I asked the two men what was wrong with the refrigerator; they said it didn't keep things cold enough. I asked if it would keep sodas cool.

"Probably okay," they said.

I thought maybe we should keep the refrigerator in our office and fill it with sodas so we didn't have to go down to the snack bar on the second floor each time we were thirsty. I suggested it to Ruth, and she agreed.

I asked the two men to bring it in. They were reluctant to do this, as they had orders to bring the old one to the loading dock to be removed. They made it clear that if this did not work out, I was responsible for removing it.

That night I went out, bought several six-packs of different kinds of soda, and brought them to the office. Before leaving, I stocked the refrigerator.

The next day our two new charges from the Philippine Navy arrived. We went down to the nursing office to meet them and then we brought them back to our office. We had planned on a little getting-to-know-you time, and then we were scheduled to bring them to lunch. Right before noon, we heard *pop, pop, pop, bang!* and on it went. I knew what had happened and so did Ruth: the cans were exploding. We started to laugh, while the two new nurses simply stared at us, not knowing what to think. Then came the loud noises from the conference room.

The doctors kept shouting, "Bomb! Bomb!" The door opened and there was a mass exodus. They couldn't get out fast enough to the elevator and stairs. Seconds later, the room was empty. All the doctors had abandoned their sandwiches—which were still on the table—and left.

I could not believe what had happened, and I could not stop laughing. Ruth was no better. I went over and opened the refrigerator door, and all the liquids dripped out onto our floor. What a sticky mess! My doing, so I cleaned. I did not want my staff involved. But getting rid of the refrigerator was a little more difficult.

Before leaving work, I brought the dolly to my office. The 3:00 P.M. to 11:00 P.M. corpsmen delivered the refrigerator to the loading dock when they went off duty. Enough of my bright ideas. When all was explained to the visiting nurses they had a few laughs, and I am sure they later told that story in the Philippines about the American nurses.

* * *

The weeks and months were going by fast. My area kept me very busy because staff were constantly changing, moving to different areas or to different duty stations. They were learning all the time, as I was. That was Navy administration. One week we had two major inspections at the same time: the Joint Commission Accreditation for Hospitals (JCAH) and the Navy Inspector General (IG). Our nursing director kept us busy, and we were all prepared. We did both inspections and passed, with excellent results.

I also returned to New Hampshire for long weekends. I could make the drive in a day. During these weekends, I checked on my sister, Ellen, who was a brittle diabetic, and on my house in

Dover, which I had purchased from my mother when I had been in Lemoore. I needed to keep an eye on it now.

It was getting time for orders. I would be sad to move on. I had lots of friends, and I liked my house and the area. Virginia was a military state, and there were lots of military around. I was happy here.

I thought, *"Maybe I will keep the house and come back after I retire when I reach twenty years."* In the meantime, I hoped I'd be assigned to the East Coast. For this to happen, a commander on the East Coast would need to be leaving about the same time I was scheduled to be reassigned; then I would be able to fill that billet. The more senior I got, the more difficult it was to be reassigned, because the billets decreased because of rank.

My orders arrived: Naval Hospital Orlando, Florida. A new hospital had been built there a few years ago, and Disney World was there. I had never been to either.

I contacted my friend Pat in Orlando who had been in California when I was there. I learned that the hospital was smaller than the one at Portsmouth. It is on the base of the Naval Recruit Training Command, Orlando Florida. The Recruit Training Center (RTC) provided basic indoctrination for enlisted Naval personnel, and it was the sole center of training for enlisted women, The other two training centers were San Diego and Great Lakes.

I didn't know the director, but we had many mutual friends, and she had been in Vietnam. There were three commanders in Orlando. I wondered, *"What will I be doing?"*

I drove down and looked around. I found a house to buy and hoped the sellers would be out when I arrived. It was going to be close. My sister was living in the house in New Hampshire, and I contacted a rental agency and made plans to rent the one in Virginia. Lots of military were looking for housing.

My area and the senior nurses gave me a party. Our group of commanders was starting to break up. I would really miss this place—it was a great group of staff.

The movers came and my household effects were shipped. I packed my car with a few last items, cleaned my house for the new tenants, and had dinner with some of my friends. I spent my final night at Ruth's house. Then, the next morning, I started driving south.

Chapter 42

Naval Hospital Orlando, Florida, 1982–1986

When I got to Florida, I went straight to Commander Pat Clancy's house. I had stayed with her in Oakland after the fire before I left for graduate school. I learned that the house I was buying wasn't vacant yet; the sellers' new home was not ready to move into and they had two small children. I had not planned on this. I would need to impose on my friend a little longer now.

Pat had a large house, so I could stay out of her way. In the past, she and her mother had stopped at my place in Virginia on their way from the Northeast to Florida. One nice thing about Navy nurses: everyone helps each other.

Since I could not move into my house, I thought I might as well check into Naval Hospital Orlando earlier and save some leave time. They could always put me to work somewhere. I let the director know I would come in a few days earlier, giving the exact date and time. I did take a couple of days before to explore different areas of the city and buy some items for my house.

I waited until late morning then went to the hospital. My first stop was the information desk so my name could be entered in the hospital log. I let them know who I was and told them that I was reporting for duty. When I gave my name, two young sailors stood up and said, "The director of nursing, Captain Lois Nickerson, wants to see you right away."

One escorted me down to her office while the other one called her office. I thought, *"What now?"*

When I arrived, she had a big smile and said, "Congratulations!"

I just looked at her. I had no idea what I was being congratulated for.

Then she added, "Captain."

It still had not registered.

Next she said, "The results of the captain selection board were released this morning."

That was one rank I had not been expecting.

"I am on the list?" I asked.

She showed it to me. I was shocked but thrilled. The next higher rank is "rear admiral," and there is only one for the Nurse Corps and one for the Reserves. I had been so involved in leaving Virginia, buying a house, and dealing with the delay, I had never thought of the board.

I then asked about my friend Pat. She had not been selected; the other two commanders stationed in Orlando, whom I did not know, had not been selected either.

"This is going to be very difficult," I said.

The director agreed and said that the news was already out and had gone through the hospital.

How could I be happy when those three were not selected? How could I stay at my friend's? It would be very awkward. My presence would be a constant reminder, and the wounds were too fresh for it not to be an issue. I really did not know how to approach her.

I thought, *"What is going to happen at the hospital with the staff assignments?"* More problems. Now I would outrank the other nurses, even though they had seniority in terms of time spent in Orlando. They had been there for years, and I was a stranger.

In the weeks ahead, I felt depressed. I received the welcome and congratulations, but if one of the three was close by, I was the new

Orlando Naval Hospital

commander reporting. I did not want the other three commanders and staff to be in a difficult position. That did not always work. They all knew who I was by then. I did stay at my friend's house but tried to be absent as much as I could. It was hard for both of us.

The captain was trying for stability and preferred not to move everyone because of me. One requested retirement, one was already expecting orders, and the third also received orders. Lois was retiring in a little over a year, and I would be taking her position. In the interim I would work in different areas and familiarize myself with the hospital. This was a four-year assignment. I had plenty of time.

NH Orlando was a medium-sized hospital and a very active one. Besides the Navy RTC on base there was also a very large population of retired personnel and snowbirds in the winter that added to the patient census. The staff consisted of Navy and civilian personnel.

I started in the clinic. Having already worked in one, I enjoyed getting to know the staff and routines. Many of the patients were returning for follow-up visits. Before I knew it, I was up in the front office as the assistant director, and I became more involved with the inpatient side.

Later I was sent to Washington to take a month-long Strategic Medical Readiness Course. I drove up with a stop in Virginia to see friends. The course was for new captains in the Medical Department from both the East Coast and the West Coast. The speakers were from the top military fields in DC; Navy War College, Newport, Rhode Island; and the civilian community. There was homework at night, and we needed to be familiar with the topics for the next day. There were only two females in this group; the other woman was a Medical Service Corps captain from the West Coast who was staying with friends.

Most of the class stayed in a hotel in Bethesda, Maryland, and the Navy provided a shuttle to take us back and forth to class. I had hoped to try a few of the restaurants while in Washington, and I overheard a small group in the class talking about them. The next day one of the doctors approached me and asked if he could borrow my car, which was large enough for a group of six. I knew what they were planning, but I asked about it anyway and told him they could use the car only if I was included. They took the deal, and I went to several places with five of my classmates. I was not going to sit in my room while they were eating out! It worked out well.

On my weekends I did a little touring around DC, including the Smithsonian Museum. At the end of our four weeks, the class had to sponsor a cocktail party at the Officers' Club for all the speakers and their spouses. I did not know that in advance. I had to find something appropriate to wear, and had only Saturday and

Sunday for shopping. At one of the larger stores, I found a dress. That was a relief.

* * *

Back in Florida, my house kept me busy also. I decided that since I was in Florida, I wanted a pool. I had to do a little research and put a fence up. I had the pool installed and then I had to know how to clean it and put the chemicals in. Soon the visitors from the north came. My house was only forty-five minutes from Disney and the other parks. I had never realized how busy you could be in the winter with people from the north.

I was introduced to the retired nurse group, which included captains and commanders. Who did I meet up with? My chief nurse from Oakland, Captain Sue Smoker, who had insisted I go for my master's degree. I also reunited in this group with Captain Ruth Halverson. She had been the ship's nurse on the *MSTS Patrick,* the ship I had returned to the states on from Vietnam. I also reconnected with many other people I had crossed paths with.

I spent several months working with Captain Nickerson. She chose a retirement date and it drew near. I helped prepare the retirement ceremony for Lois. It is a large celebration when a senior nurse retires. There was a dinner the night before the ceremony, the retirement ceremony, a big party after the retirement ceremony at the Officers' Club, and then a smaller party after that. Several of Lois's friends were flying in, as well as many Vietnam nurses. My house was full.

Lois had a great retirement celebration and sendoff. Two days later, her movers packed her household goods for her move back to Texas. I knew I would miss her. She was an excellent nursing director, and I enjoyed working for her. She was also a good friend. I had been fortunate that most of my directors were excellent, and I did learn something from each of them.

On Monday morning I reported to the commanding officer as Director of Nursing Services. I had moved my things into my new office, and the new assistant moved into my old one. There would be no more changes at work for a while.

* * *

I decided to get a new car. I had been thinking of it for months. Lois had been telling me I should buy a Thunderbird, and I bought one in silver. It was parked close to the commanding officer's office, and he could see it from his window.

The next morning, he said, "Whose car is that?" I explained that it was mine.

Two weeks later I had problems with my new car, so in it went for repairs. I had a loaner, and once again the commanding officer asked, "Whose car is that?"

I explained that it was my loaner.

I got my car back for a while, but three weeks later I had another loaner because of more problems with my car. The commanding officer kept wondering what was going on with all these cars. I was very upset, because each day that I had a loner I had to go for a visitor pass, which caused a delay.

After morning report, they would discuss my car problem, and someone suggested that I should check the Florida Lemon Law for cars. Good idea. At the time, I had my own car back, so I thought I was safe. Then one morning as I was going to work on the highway, with cars all around me, the hood popped open and I could not see in front of me. I knew that if I put on my brakes, there would be a massive pileup. I was in the middle lane, and the other cars were all blowing their horns. I could not see my turnoff and needed to get in the other lane.

I thought, *"If I get out of this alive, I am going to sue that dealership!"*

The cars on both sides kept moving along, so I moved with them. Then the one on the right turned off and I was able to move into his lane. A few minutes later I knew my turnoff was coming up, so I slowed down for the ramp. I pulled to the side and stopped. I put the hood down and made it to the base. One of the men at work checked it for me.

I told the commanding officer that after work I was going to the dealership and I was going to get a new car, using the Lemon Law. I went to the dealership, and there were several salespeople with customers who were looking at cars. I asked to see the manager. I had already been there several times, and they could see I was angry. They told me he was not there, but I could see he was in his office. I was in my Navy uniform with my shoulder boards and four gold stripes. They had not seen me in this uniform before.

I told two of them that if I didn't get to speak with the manager in a couple of minutes, I was going to go over to the people looking at cars and tell them not to buy here. They had sold me a new defective car, and they couldn't repair it. I would also put notices up on the base to warn people to stay away from there. The manager came, and I told him I wanted a new car or I would use the Lemon Law and the base would be made aware of this place.

Since I had the documentation, I had a new car the next day. As soon as it was in my name, I turned it in at another dealership for another new car. I did not want a car from the original dealership.

I thought, *"It seems that almost everywhere I go, I have a car problem."* Well, that problem was finally solved, and since that time, I have had several new cars of the same make with no problems.

* * *

One day, when I had been at NH Orlando around three years, both the commanding officer and the executive officer were away, so I was the senior officer. A nurse from the ER called to see if I could come down; they had a problem. I went right down. She met me in the hall and said that a Marine Corps general had been brought in by his two aides, but he would not let anyone examine him or answer any questions. The ER doctor was a lieutenant commander, and the general wanted to see someone with authority. I asked for the general's name. The younger staff had not recognize it, but I immediately did. I had never met him, but he was well known and highly decorated.

The general had been retired for some time, and I suspected that his aides were probably attendants because he came from a retirement facility in another state. I was in my summer white uniform with shoulder boards. Time to meet the general. I walked in, approached him, and introduced myself.

I said, "I'm Captain Reynolds, Director of Nursing Services, and I am filling in for the commanding officer and the executive officer. Do I have enough authority?"

I had taken his wrist to check his pulse. He glanced at my shoulder boards and then looked at my ribbons.

He said, "What's that?"

I knew he was looking at the Purple Heart, so I said, "General you know what that is! You have a couple of them!"

He said, "Of course I know what that is. Where did you get it?"

I said, "You know those ribbons also."

He grinned.

I told him what the doctor and nurse were going to do. I then said, "Is that okay with you?"

He replied with a quiet "Yes."

I said, "I am going to hold your hand while the team is working on you." Then I sent his aides (attendants) to the cafeteria.

While he was being treated, I told him about my bombing to answer his questions. Since the hospital was quiet, I was able to spend some time with him. The ER held him for several hours, and then he was able to return to his nursing home.

* * *

The Navy Hospital provided two ambulances when there was a Space Shuttle launch at Cape Canaveral. Nurses and hospital corpsmen rode in the ambulances to help with crowd control and be on hand for any accidents. The teams left very early in the morning to set up. The vehicles were parked up front and the teams had a perfect view of the shuttle launch.

The base had a good view also. On January 28, 1986, I went outside to watch one. This was a special launch, because a schoolteacher, Christa McAuliffe from New Hampshire, was on it, and there had been a lot of press. Everyone who could stand outside had gathered. Radios and TVs were on.

The shuttle went up, we watched, and then we waited. We all know now what happened. I was standing with several people, and we were in shock. I had seen several launches, but not an ending like this. The Space Shuttle *Challenger* exploded with a huge fireball, killing all seven crew members—a day many will always remember.

* * *

In terms of the general work environment, the nursing department was not having any difficulties. Then the commanding officer

retired and a new one reported. The Navy was changing the leadership of the top administrators. Instead of a physician as commanding officer, it would be a medical service officer. Our hospital would
be one of the first to try this. I was in for many headaches. Patient
care was my top priority, with my staff running a tie. The new commanding officer had lots of ideas for nursing, but we did not have
the staff and could not hire. Our personnel numbers were decided
either by the Bureau or the budget. Trying times. I also received
orders from Washington to sit on captain and commander selection
boards and conferences. I was busy.

* * *

There were always a few challenges for the nursing department.
I had the JCAH and the Navy IG team for inspections. (At least
they were not on the same day like they had been in Portsmouth.)
The nursing department did well, and I was sent to another military
hospital to help them prepare for an inspection. I was also sent to
one to sit on a board of inquiry, a step before a court martial. That
was interesting, and the case involved drugs.

I thought it would be good to have an educational program
on drugs and have NCIS (Naval Criminal Investigative Service)
present it. The commanding officer was aware of the program. I
asked the agents to bring marijuana/cannabis so the nurses could
be familiar with it. Some were not. They all were able to examine
and smell it.

When the odor escaped under the door into the hall, everyone suddenly wanted to know what the nurses were doing. I was
glad we had NCIS there. Anyone caught using a drug could be
discharged from the military.

* * *

Then came the bomb scares. The first call made to the hospital warned that a bomb was set to go off later that morning. NCIS was called. We were told to evacuate the entire hospital. It was a challenge for staff to keep ICU and ward patients calm. The OR staff volunteered to stay and finish the procedures in the OR and then they and the patients also came out. It was a very hot day with very little shade.

After several hours, the hospital was cleared to bring the patients back. In the middle of the afternoon there was another call, and again all patients had to be removed. Someone was playing games with the hospital staff. After more inspections, all patients were brought back in. It was a lot of hard work moving patients, beds, cribs, equipment, and so forth.

Once we had everything back to normal, I went home. At 9:30 p.m., another call came and I went back to the hospital. This time NCIS told us not to evacuate. They thought they knew who was doing it, so they told us just to send a few people out so the person under investigation would stay engaged. They caught a Navy recruit who was making the calls in the barracks. He was punished. The staff were well trained on moving patients.

* * *

Next there was a new commanding officer for the base. Our commanding officer thought he might be able to make some changes now. The rear admiral decided to come to the hospital every Friday to visit all the recruits who were hospitalized. Then he planned to stop for a short time in my commanding officer's office. The admiral always included me with the recruit visits and the informal meetings in the CO's office after. There was no private time for my commanding officer—no hospital discussions.

During our informal meetings, the subjects tended to focus on world situations and books. The first time I met the admiral, I was not prepared to take part in a discussion. The admiral said he was reading the book *The Hunt for Red October*. He was a submarine officer, and he knew the author, Tom Clancy. After work that day, I bought the book. I needed to be ready for next week's meeting. Those discussions were always interesting.

One of the extra duties I had was to inspect the recruit barracks. The captains on base would share this duty. The recruits were always surprised to see a female captain—even more so when I opened their lockers and found interesting posters of female models.

The admiral was there two years then retired. There was a Change of Command ceremony, which is always impressive, and I had a front-row seat with my commanding officer.

About six months later, my CO retired because he had a good offer to be the administrator of a hospital in Saudi Arabia. Another six months or so passed, and he came back to visit. He was looking for a nursing director and nurses for his hospital. He knew I had my time in for captain and asked if I would go and be the director of nurses in Saudi Arabia. The money was very good, but my answer was no.

* * *

My four years would end soon. I had completed the twenty years I had planned. Did I want to retire? I wasn't sure. There were rumors about the Middle East. The hospital ship was coming out.

Would I be interested in working on that? No. What about the Director of Nursing position at Camp Lejeune? A new hospital had opened there two years earlier. When I had been there as an ensign, I had said it would take a pack of wild horses to get me back there again. Now, though, I thought about it. I was a captain, and the position would last a couple of years and put my time of service over twenty-six years. I could retire from there. I could rent out my house in Florida and rent another home near Camp Lejeune. I agreed to return to the Marine Corps base.

My orders arrived. Time to pack again. I called my friends Anne and Betty, two Navy nurses who had retired in Jacksonville, North Carolina, to let them know I had orders there. I asked them to keep an eye out for houses to rent. The Navy chief who was assigned to the nursing department had been at Camp Lejeune before and gave me lots of advice. He added, "Make sure your ribbons are always correct. The Marines might question them."

Shortly before I moved to North Carolina, the ER called and said there was a general who wanted to see me. When I saw him, I said, "General! You missed me and came back."

He had failed in that year. I told him I had orders to one of his favorite places, Marine Corps Base Camp Lejeune. He seemed pleased to hear it. He was a very popular, well-liked Marine who now appears in history books. Another very interesting patient.

We treated him and sent him back to Mississippi. A few weeks later, I packed my things and headed for Camp Lejeune.

Chapter 43

Naval Hospital Camp Lejeune
North Carolina, 1986

I drove north for my next assignment. I had not been to Camp Lejeune since 1963. I was sure I would not recognize the place. I guess I just wanted to prove something to myself. I had always said I would never return, but there I was. I had renters for my house, an agency to watch it, and neighbors to keep an eye on it. I planned to move back to Florida after I retired.

I'd been invited to stay with Anne and Betty until I found a place. Anne, now a retired captain, was the recruiter in Boston who had received the dispatch orders to Da Nang. Betty was also a Vietnam nurse but had been assigned south of Saigon. She was also a retired captain and had been the director of nursing at Camp Lejeune in the old hospital a few years back.

They had a very large house, so I wouldn't be in their way. I had a couple of days to look for my own house, so the next day I took a tour of the area, the base, the hospital, and the city of Jacksonville. There had been many changes. My last stop was the housing office. Then I started off on my own and went back to the referral section. I told them who I was and what I was looking for.

They said a house had just become available that morning. I looked at a photo and the price and said I wanted to see it. They gave me the key and directions. I liked it. It was a mirror image of my brick ranch in Virginia. I went back and asked my friends to come look because they knew the houses in the area. The timing was good. I could rent it for three years, at which point the owner, who was now at Camp Pendleton, would be returning. I could move right in. Housing was settled. Anne and Betty offered to be there when my furniture was delivered, and I would unpack boxes later.

The next day I reported for duty. The present director was retiring in a very short time. There was a lot of information to cover. This hospital was larger than NH Orlando, and some things were a little different because it was part of a Marine Corps Base. Just seeing everyone in different uniforms with ranks and rates by different names was a change from the Navy. (See the chart of military ranks in the appendix.)

I met the commanding officer, who was retiring in a few weeks, and the executive officer, a Nurse Corps officer who had orders. Then I met the rest of the staff. I had only been there a few weeks when the new commanding officer, Captain M., reported. He was a young man who had been a flight surgeon, with no recent experience with hospital management. This would be interesting. I also learned that the secretary for the Nursing department was leaving in a few weeks.

The commanders wanted to hire the new secretary themselves. I thought about it and asked if they had criteria. They said yes, so I let them. It was an excellent teaching exercise. The first secretary had difficulty in the position and lasted about five weeks. The next one did not work out either, because her husband had orders and she left. I said I was doing the next interviews and the hiring. I had two commanders with me to educate them on the hiring process. The candidate I interviewed was middle-aged and came from the Marine Corps side of the base, which we also called the green side of the base. I hired her, and she was an outstanding secretary for the entire department. In fact, the other departments wanted to steal her away from us. Fortunately, Rosemary was loyal to the nursing department.

Darby

The hospital was new, and we had one ward that we could not utilize due to a lack of staffing. This was usually empty. The staff used it for PFT (Physical Fitness Training). There was a lot of training on the base.

Each day I attended morning report with all the department heads in the hospital and the Navy senior people from the Marine side. I was always there several minutes before the commanding officer to get a heads up on any nursing problems. No matter what, Captain M. would never start the report without me. The green side had many training exercises, and the hospital was notified ahead because some were live fire.

My duties were the same as at Orlando, but our patient population was mostly active duty and retired Marines, plus their dependents. Staff was both military and civilian. If the commanding officer or executive officer were not on board, I answered to the base general.

* * *

The commanding officer decided he wanted all department heads to have their photographs taken in full uniform, with covers (hats). The photos would be placed on a wall in the lobby. This was a very busy area, because the Marines waited there for transportation to take them back to their work areas. Finally, the photos were up. The waiting Marines found this wall very interesting as they could see who the staff were. Our ribbons showed some of the areas we had been assigned to, and any awards.

Since I was a captain and the only female on the wall, I knew my photo would draw attention. One day Rosemary, my secretary, came to me with a grin on her face and said I had to take a call. I asked her why. She said, "Just take the call."

With her still grinning, I knew something had her interest. I answered and identified myself. A young Marine gave me his name and said, "I've been looking at the photos and noticed you have your ribbons on wrong." Then I remembered that my chief in Orlando had said I might be questioned. I thought, *"Here it is."*

I asked what ribbon, and he said, "First one. The good conduct one. It belongs further down."

I looked at Rosemary; she was leaning in the doorway laughing. I almost laughed myself. I did not have a good conduct ribbon. Officers were expected to display good conduct, although if you had been enlisted, you might have had this ribbon. At that point I told him it was not the Good Conduct Ribbon but the Purple Heart. Dead silence. I waited as I thought he might have hung up.

He came back and said he had not known that women could receive the Purple Heart. At that point he received a mini-talk on women in the military. Not only did they receive Purple Hearts, but two nurse friends of mine stationed at Da Nang had earned the Bronze Star with Combat V. Later I said to Rosemary, "That's the end of that." She said no, and the next day a reporter from the base newspaper called; she wanted an interview. I was caught again. The article and picture were in the base newspaper. It did educate the Marines.

My commanding officer often came up with ideas for training, but most were not feasible with our patients as subjects. In morning report, the other members of our group frequently asked me to explain why we could not do certain things. They liked to give me the problem, because they did not want to get on his wrong side. I was all for training but refused some of the proposals. Safety first. Whenever an idea seemed questionable, I talked to him and explained it.

The medical group was having problems. Following morning reports, I went back to my commanders to give them an update on things they needed to know. One day I told them I felt like a witch. It was around Halloween, and one commander said, "Why don't you go to a morning meeting dressed as a witch?"

They were laughing. She actually had the costume to take her children out trick-or-treating. I thought about it and decided it might change the atmosphere. So, I dressed up like a witch in the morning. Conveniently, the nurses were having a food sale that day in the lobby to raise money for food baskets at Thanksgiving, so I also had a plastic pumpkin full of brownies.

I waited to enter until after everyone had arrived, because I was sure they would not start the report without me. The commanding officer asked his secretary to find out where I was. With broom and pumpkin, I made my entrance and swept all the papers off the table. As I did so, I said, "There are enough bad vibes coming out of the room. It needs a clean sweep!"

They didn't know who the witch was at first. They were too busy retrieving their papers from the floor and laughing. I then went around again and gave out the brownies. Things were much better for a time.

* * *

One day, I decided to pay a visit to the Marine side of the base to check their first aid stations. Navy corpsmen were assigned there to treat Marines with minor problems. Major problems were sent to the hospital, The first aid stations were also responsible for making sure that all Marines were ready for deployment and all immunizations were up to date and recorded correctly in the health records. These corpsmen would go with the units if shipped out. They needed to be ready also.

I found the aid station and went up the steps. A corpsman and a Marine were sitting with their feet on the desk. The Marine saw me and jumped to his feet; then the corpsman did the same. The Marine said he had to leave. The hospital corpsman, petty officer second class, was not there.

I did a low-key inspection and began teaching the junior corpsman about procedures. When I was almost finished, the petty officer second class came rushing in. I told him to pass the word that I would be back. There was a lot to inspect, and education was needed. There were several other stations, but I would not tell him where or when I would arrive next—I just told them to be ready. I felt they needed a nurse on the Marine side to supervise and educate. The command request was generated, and a Navy nurse was assigned from the detailer in Washington before I retired.

The next time I went out to the Marine side and was at an aid station talking with the corpsman, a civilian nurse came in and asked the corpsman a question. I asked where she worked on base, and she said, "I am a school nurse."

There were five schools. This was a very large base with many dependents and school children. (High school students took the bus to the high school off base.) Each school on the base had a nurse. I asked her who she was responsible to.

She said, "The director of nursing at the hospital." I introduced myself and told her I knew nothing about this. This turned into another problem. The Marine Corps hired these nurses and paid their salary, but nursing at the hospital was responsible to make sure that their licenses and other requirements were up to date. I had found two problems by deciding to leave the hospital to make rounds in the green side.

* * *

I made a couple of trips to Washington to take part in a selection board and to attend a course with other senior nurses. Work kept me busy, but in my free time I would often see Anne and Betty. There were a few other retired Navy nurses in the area and others who would stop by their home when traveling. I also tried sailing.

The base had cottages at the beach for officers and enlisted. One was designated for the colonel/captain. To reserve this cottage, you had to pick a date, put your name in a lottery, and wait for the date of the draw to see if you had a win. I went over to the office and asked if I could put my name in. The office staff did not know if I could do this. I told them I was a Navy captain, same as a Marine colonel. (See the chart of military ranks in the appendix.)

My name went in and I won a weekend. I decided to go look at it. Since it was on base I drove there, but on my way back I was suddenly stopped by Marines all painted and in camouflage. They came out of the woods and pointed their weapons at me.

I was in the middle of an exercise, and I had entered the live fire zone. They had to stop the exercise, and more men came out from the trees to make sure I did leave the area. I had missed the sign. That was an exciting morning. I never was able to spend time at the cottage. A hurricane prevented the next try.

* * *

Time was moving on, and my health became an issue. I was so tired I could hardly get myself to work. I went through many tests and procedures. Then I met with a new physician and had more tests. A diagnosis was made and a trip to Bethesda was scheduled for treatment. It was my thyroid. I felt better already just knowing the problem.

After several months had gone by, I woke up one morning and decided that I had put my twenty-six years in. I had always said if I couldn't be a role model and keep up with the PFTs (Physical Fitness Tests), it was time to leave. I requested to retire on May 20, 1988. I let the executive officer know, and he would inform the commanding officer. First they tried to talk me out of it. I gave the nursing division my date of request so they would have several months to name my relief.

The next few months went by, and there was more unrest with the physicians. Soon there would be a visit from the Surgeon General (SG) of the Navy, and he would meet with the physicians. Since I had been stationed and worked with the SG in the operating room several years before, I expected to be on his list of people he would see. The SG made his visit and met with all the physicians regarding their concerns. There were no decisions at this time, but I wondered if they would be announced and implemented before or after my retirement. That was fast approaching.

I had to name the guest speaker for my retirement program. I knew who I would like but didn't know if she would come or even be available. My choice was Rear Admiral Mary J. Nielubowicz Nurse Corps, USN (retired), immediate past Director of the Navy Nurse Corps. She had been my director of nursing when I was a commander stationed at Portsmouth, Virginia. I called and asked the Rear Admiral, and she accepted.

There was a lot to think about. Commander Tish Breeding asked if she could be in charge of the ceremonies for my retirement, which was a big relief for me.

Immediately before my official retirement date, I was taking thirty days terminal leave. I made arrangements so that a few days after my retirement, the movers would come and I would move back to Orlando. I would have a full house before my retirement, and some guests were staying after for a couple of days.

My relief, a captain, had not reported yet, and we learned that there would be a three-month delay. I had not expected that. The senior commander would fill in for that time. I felt she was capable because there would not be any changes in procedures; any major decisions would be postponed until there was a new director.

For my last morning report, I decided to do something to give the group another laugh. I asked one of the male nurses to find a flak jacket and a helmet. I also prepared a tray of brownies to go with their coffee. When they were all in their seats, I went in wearing the outfit and told them it was their last chance to throw things at me. I was ready!

That night, the hospital staff had a dinner for me. The rear admiral was there, along with my sister and several friends from around the country. It was a roast. The nurses had put together a skit, composing funny words for the music, and they had made outfits from old parachute material.

The next afternoon was warm and sunny. My retirement ceremony was held outside by the flagpole. Admiral Nielubowicz was the speaker, the Marine Corps General and the Marine Corps band were also there, and then my reception followed.

That night was a catered pig roast, and the following night Anne and Betty had a party for me. I certainly had a wonderful retirement, and I was grateful to CDR Breeding and her helpers.

Naval Hospital Camp Lejeune

1988 retirement ceremony, Camp Lejeune

Retirement party with
Rear Admiral Mary J. Nielubowicz, Nurse Corps, USN (retired)

Retirement party with Captain Sue Smoker and Captain Ruth Halverson

Retirement party with Darby's sister, Ellen

Rosemary and Darby at retirement dinner

* * *

My company left and the movers came. My household goods were on the way to Florida. I had someone help me clean. The owners would be moving back early and were already on their way.

I was anxious to return to Florida and get settled. The movers delivered my things two days later. Three days later, I was in the middle of unpacking when the phone rang. It was the personnel office at Camp Lejeune.

The personnel officer said, "Captain Reynolds, I regret I have to tell you this, but you have been recalled to duty."

I said, "I'm retired."

He said, "No, you're not. You are on terminal leave."

I said, "Okay. I'm on leave."

He said, "It's cancelled."

I said, "You can't do this."

He said, "The commanding officer can."

I forgot that my commanding officer had been transferred to

a smaller hospital. The new commanding officer was onboard. All legal.

I asked him how soon I had to be there. He said, "Tomorrow."

I said, "Impossible. I'll need to close my house, pack my uniforms, and make the drive."

I said I'd be there the day after. Then I asked, "What happened?"

He wouldn't give me a direct reply. He said I would find out when I got there.

I could not imagine what could have happened to put this chain of events in motion; rarely does this occur. I called Anne and Betty and asked if they had heard anything. No. I asked them to make a reservation for me in the BOQ. They invited me to stay with them instead.

I said, "Fine—at least until I find out what is going on."

I closed up the house and asked the neighbors to keep an eye on my place. When I arrived in Jacksonville, I called Rosemary. She said she was sorry I had needed to come back but was glad I was returning.

When I asked what was going on, she said, "Wait and see. Come in around 8:10."

I was still in the dark and couldn't imagine what might be happening.

I arrived at the hospital and stopped by the personnel office to be checked back off leave. I had been gone a little over a week. The personnel officer told me to take care of a problem in the nursing department.

I said, "What problem?"

He said, "It will be very obvious. Just take care of it."

This was not sounding good.

I went down to the nursing department and walked in. Rosemary was sitting at her desk. She pointed to my office. I opened my door and saw the husband of one of my nurses sitting in the chair. He was a retired Navy chief. He had his feet up on my desk and didn't look up from the newspaper he was reading.

He said, "You're back early."

Clearly he thought I was his wife. I pulled the newspaper away and said, "You are right. I am back."

He looked at me and said, "What are you doing here?"

I said, "I came back to clean out my office, and if you are not gone by the time I count to ten, I will have security remove you."

He said, "You can't do that! My wife is in charge!"

I said, "Look again! I am back. I have the eagle and I am in charge."

He continued to argue. He now thought he was in charge.

I told Rosemary that I needed security right away to escort someone from my office. I added that they might need two men. I explained that the retired Navy chief was not to come back to the nursing department, and that unless he had a medical appointment they would need to remove him from the hospital. His wife, the commander, was no longer in charge.

By then the wife had returned. I think she thought I was a ghost.

I told her what I told the husband, emphasizing that I was back and would talk with her later. Security arrived, and they escorted him to the front door. He was furious and still had a few more words for me. I think he thought he could run the nursing department and had been telling his wife what to do.

Now to find out how this started and take care of the problem. I had a meeting with all of the commanders. The problem involved three nurses and the husband. The four of them had been trying to change the nursing department before the new nursing director reported, and the new commanding officer did not want this to happen. He had enough problems without a nursing one. It was not a good way for him to start in a new command. I was told that I would need to remain in my position until September, when the new captain would finally be reporting.

It was another busy time. I had over two months and fitness reports needed to be updated. The commanding officer had to sign the finalized reports. New assignments would come from the detailer in the Nurse Corps Division in Washington.

My friends wanted me to continue staying at their house, and I agreed. It was a lot nicer than the BOQ on base and I was able to get away a few weekends. I had received orders to be in Washington for a meeting right after July 4, so I went up early and stayed with CDR Tish Breeding. She had been transferred to Washington in early June. We went to the Parade and to the Capitol Fourth of July Concert. The concert and fireworks were great, and it was a wonderful opportunity to be there on the Fourth of July.

I returned to Camp Lejeune and worked with the new commanding officer on the few changes he wanted. Time went by quickly. The new director of nursing services reported for duty and I stayed four days to orient her. Then I returned to Florida as a retiree.

Awards and Decorations:

Purple Heart; Two Meritorious Service Medals; Combat Action Ribbon; Navy Unit Commendation; Meritorious Unit Commendation; National Defense Service Medal; Vietnam Service Medal; Republic of Vietnam Meritorious Unit Citation (Gallantry Cross Color); Republic of Vietnam; Meritorious Unit Citation (Civil Action Color); Republic of Vietnam Campaign Medal

* * *

One topic I did not touch on in this book is Post-Traumatic Stress Disorder (PTSD). Many of the Vietnam nurses came back with it and never knew they had it. Many have difficult memories that do not go away, and nurses handle it differently. Some will admit it; others will not. One nurse described it as putting all the memories in a paper bag; eventually the bag will burst or compartmentalize. Since Vietnam and our current wars, so much more has been discovered about PTSD and treatments that are now available for the active duty, veterans, and civilians. Hopefully they will be utilized.

* * *

My Navy career had finally come to an end, but the twenty-six and a half years on active duty had given me so many adventures, challenges, and rewards. There were some hardships along the way, and Vietnam was the most memorable, for me and for many of the nurses. Our experiences depended on which branch of service we belonged to, which part of the country we were sent to, and which years we were there. The one constant was the patients.

For each experience I've described in the book—or adventure, as I refer to them—I have shared some of my knowledge, but I gained so much more. The largest gift has been the friendships, which have lasted for years. I am grateful for them all.

Epilogue

I spent a few months in my Florida home and began thinking about going back to work or becoming a volunteer. I was approached about two work positions. One was in central Florida with the American Red Cross, and the other one, which required quite a bit of traveling, was with the JCAH (Joint Commission Accreditation for Hospitals). However, before I made a decision, my sister went into the hospital, so I returned to New Hampshire. I was there for several weeks, then back to Florida for a few months, and then back to New Hampshire again. This back and forth went on for some time, and then my elderly aunts started having problems. Since I was involved with three relatives' care, I decided to move back North.

In New Hampshire, my volunteer work became a full-time activity. Into the mix, I had the care of my sister's aging cockapoo. I eventually sold my homes in Florida and Virginia because I knew I would not return permanently to either location.

On Veterans Day, 1993, I was able to go to Virginia to visit some friends and attend the dedication of the Vietnam Women's Memorial in Washington, DC. It was also a reunion for the Navy nurses, and it was wonderful to see so many old friends. I remember marching down Constitution Avenue with the nurses and women from all branches of the military to the dedication, then walking around the memorial several times. There were hundreds of people trying to get close to the memorial. I heard a woman call out, "Does anyone know my aunt? She was a Navy nurse. I have her picture."

I was not close to the woman, but I was able to glance at the photograph as she was holding it above her head. I thought I recognized the nurse, who was in dress blues in the photograph, but before I could reach the woman, I was caught in the

Display at the Woodman Museum in Dover, New Hampshire

crowd. Eventually I did meet up with her and said, "I did know your aunt, Ann O. She was in my apartment in Boston." I had learned several years before that Ann had died with cancer. The woman, who was with her niece, was in tears. They had traveled from Massachusetts hoping to find someone who might know Ann. I pulled her out of the crowd and found some of my friends, and we were all able to tell the niece some stories about her aunt. A few more tears were shed. Then we visited the Vietnam Wall. The entire weekend was an emotional one for everyone.

Back in New Hampshire, my volunteer work kept me extremely busy. My sister's cockerpoo had to be put down, but after a short period of time the house felt too quiet, and my sister needed company. We adopted a cockapoo puppy named Benji, (who was fourteen years old when his time came). I went back to a cycle of nursing visits, doctor visits, nursing home visits, and funerals. I had Benji and my garden to keep me occupied. Then one day I received a visit from Judy and Jim Lynch with a beautiful handmade quilt of valor made by Judy. It was a short time before her death with cancer.

I gave several media interviews and did a few talks about Vietnam. My uniform and medals were donated to the Woodman Museum in Dover, New Hampshire.

I received the Alumni Award of Merit from Saint Anselm College, and the Daughters of the American Revolution (DAR) presented me with the DAR Distinguished Citizen Medal for the State of New Hampshire, and a Quilt of Valor. The Warrior Canine Connection has named a black lab puppy with my name, Darby. After two years of training, she will be assigned to a wounded veteran as a service dog.

As the years flew by, I decided to move to an Accredited Continuing Care Retirement Community (CCRC) called RiverWoods, Exeter in Exeter, New Hampshire. Then, after several years, I was finally convinced to put some of my travels to paper. At the moment, a world event called the Coronavirus (COVID-19) is taking place. That could be a book of its own. Thankfully, to date the excellent management has kept the virus from entering our doors.

I am grateful to everyone who supported my journey through the Navy and beyond. You have helped me create a life full of memories!

MILITARY RANK OFFICERS

Navy / Coast Guard

01	Ensign	ENS	
02	Lieutenant Junior Grade	Ltjg	
03	Lieutenant	LT	
04	Lieutenant Commander	LCDR	
05	Commander	CDR	
06	Captain	CAPT	
07	Rear Admiral (lower half)	RADM	1 star
08	Rear Admiral (upper half)	RADM	2 star
09	Vice Admiral	VADM	3 star
0-10	Admiral	ADM	4 star

0-10—Chief of Naval Operations
Commandant of the Coast Guard
0-11   Fleet Admiral 5 star (wartime use)

MILITARY RANK OFFICERS

		Army	Marine Corps	Air Force	
01	Second Lieutenant	2nd LT	2nd Lt	2nd Lt	
02	First Lieutenant	1st LT	1st Lt	1st Lt	
03	Captain	CPT	Capt	Capt	
04	Major	MAJ	Maj	Maj	
05	Lieutenant Colonel	LTC	LtCol	LtCol	
06	Colonel	COL	Col.	Col	
07	Brigadier General	BG	BrigGen	Brig Gen	1 star
08	Major General	MG	MajGen	MajGen	2 star
09	Lieutenant General	LTG	LtGen	LtGen	3 star
0-10	General	GEN	Gen	Gen	4 star

0-10—Army, Chief of Staff
   Commandant of Marine Corps
   Air Force Chief of Staff
0-11   Five Star

References

"Exeter Resident Captain Ann 'Darby' Reynolds Receives Alumni Award from Saint Anselm College." readMedia, November 27, 2013. http://readme.readmedia.com/Exeter-Resident-Captain-Ann-Darby-Reynolds-Receives-Alumni-Award-from-Saint-Anselm-College/7513867.

"For God and Country." *Portraits: The Magazine of Saint Anselm College,* November 7, 2016. http://blogs.anselm.edu/portraits/features/for-god-and-country/.

Ford, Daniel. *The Only War We've Got.* Lincoln, NE: Author's Choice Press, 2001.

Gearhiser, Patrick, Petty Officer 2nd Class. "All Hands Update: Female Vietnam Purple Heart Recipient." Defense Media Activity. Accessed December 10, 2020. https://www.dvidshub.net/video/109252/all-hands-update-female-vietnam-purple-heart-recipient.

Herman, Jan K. *Naval Medicine in Vietnam: Passage to Freedom to the Fall of Saigon. Washington, DC: Naval History & Heritage Command,* nd. Accessed December 10, 2020. https://www.history.navy.mil/content/dam/nhhc/research/publications/Publication-PDF/NavyMedicine.pdf.

Herman, Jan K. *Navy Medicine in Vietnam: Oral Histories from Dien Bien Phu to the Fall of Saigon.* Jefferson, NC: McFarland, 2008.

Hovis, Bobbi, LCDR, Nurse Corps USN (Ret.). *Station Hospital Saigon: A Navy Nurse in Vietnam 1963–1964.* Annapolis, MD: United States Naval Institute Press, 1991.

Ibach, Maryanne Gallagher, RADM, USNR, comp. *Memories of Navy Nursing: The Vietnam Era.* Accessed December 10, 2020. http://www.vietnamwomensmemorial.org/pdf/magallagher.pdf.

"Join Us in Welcoming WCC's Darby." Warrior Canine Connection. Accessed December 10, 2020. https://www.facebook.com/WarriorCanineConnection/posts/join-us-in-welcoming-wccs-darby-named-in-honor-of-united-states-navy-nurse-corps/2359533690790881/.

Keefe, Jennifer. "Rare Purple Heart Recipient Wishes Troops Well." *Foster's Daily Democrat, Dec 19, 2010.* https://www.fosters.com/article/20101219/GJNEWS_01/712199882.

National Purple Heart Hall of Honor. Accessed December 11, 2020. https://www.thepurpleheart.com/roll-of-honor/profile/default?rID=38a76a71-141c-45e6-906d-745ed6ec7c69.

Naval History and Heritage Command. "Lieutenant (junior grade) Anne Darby Reynolds and Christmas Eve 1964 in Saigon." Friday, December 24, 2010. https://www.navalhistory.org/2010/12/24/lieutenant-junior-grade-anne-darby-reynolds-and-christmas-eve-1964-in-saigon.

"Navy Nurse Honored with Vietnam Vets." *New Hampshire Nursing News,* July 2016. https://d3ms3kxrsap50t.cloudfront.net/uploads/publication/pdf/1369/New_Hampshire_7_16_WEB.pdf.

Pullen, Alicia. "Navy Nurses in Saigon." Hampton Roads Naval Museum, May 15, 2020. https://hamptonroadsnavalmuseum.blogspot.com/2020/05/navy-nurses-in-saigon.html.

Sadler, Barry S/SGT with Tom Mahoney. *I'm a Lucky One.* New York: Macmillan, 1967.

Smith, Mikelle, MC3. "My Purple Heart: One Vietnam Veteran's Story of Survival." *All Hands.* March 2011, no. 1128. https://www.moaa-nh.org/All_Hands_(Mar_11).pdf.

Sterner, Doris M., Captain, Nurse Corps, USN (Ret.). *In and Out of Harm's Way: A History of the Navy Nurse Corps.* Peanut Butter Publishing, 1996.

Stur, Heather Marie, Ph.D. "U.S. Women Got Purple Hearts in Vietnam." May 20, 2017. https://hmstur.wordpress.com/2017/05/20/u-s-women-got-purple-hearts-in-vietnam/.

"TREASURE #21: Dover Woman First to Receive Purple Heart in Vietnam." *Foster's Daily Democrat*, May 11, 2016. https://www.fosters.com/article/20160511/NEWS/160519781.

Wise, James E., Jr. and Scott Baron. *Women at War: Iraq, Afghanistan, and Other Conflicts.* Annapolis, MD: Naval Institute Press, 2011.

Made in United States
Orlando, FL
27 March 2023

31468418R00167